SpringerBriefs in Education

More information about this series at http://www.springer.com/series/8914

Steve McCarty · Takeshi Sato
Hiroyuki Obari

Implementing Mobile Language Learning Technologies in Japan

Springer

Steve McCarty
Osaka Jogakuin University
Osaka
Japan

Hiroyuki Obari
Aoyama Gakuin University
Tokyo
Japan

Takeshi Sato
Tokyo University of Agriculture
and Technology
Tokyo
Japan

ISSN 2211-1921 ISSN 2211-193X (electronic)
SpringerBriefs in Education
ISBN 978-981-10-2449-8 ISBN 978-981-10-2451-1 (eBook)
DOI 10.1007/978-981-10-2451-1

Library of Congress Control Number: 2016950369

Printed on acid-free paper

This Springer imprint is published by Springer Nature
The registered company is Springer Nature Singapore Pte Ltd.
The registered company address is: 152 Beach Road, #22-06/08 Gateway East, Singapore 189721, Singapore

Contents

About the Authors

Steve McCarty was born in Boston and specialized in Japan Studies at the University of Hawaii. He was a regular faculty member in Japan during 1985–2015 (Full Professor from 1993). As of 2016, he is a Lecturer at Osaka Jogakuin University, Kansai University, and the Kobe Institute of Computing Graduate School of Information Technology. He also lectures for the Japan International Cooperation Agency of the Japanese government, introducing Japan to officials from nearly 200 countries since 2004. He is the elected President of the academic NGO World Association for Online Education (WAOE, www.waoe.org) since 1998.

He started global networking with a Japanese-English homepage in 1996, an online e-portfolio from 1997, and video on the Web in 1998, 7 years before YouTube. He started using learning management systems in 1999. He pioneered a globally accessible mobile Internet site in the year 2000. He has delivered keynote addresses at several international e-learning conferences. Google Scholar has found nearly 200 citations to his writings. Most of his more than 250 publications, including presentations, as well as podcasts, videos, social media, and other Websites are linked from his bilingual e-portfolio: www.waoe.org/steve/epublist.html.

Dr. Hiroyuki Obari is Professor in the College of Economics at Aoyama Gakuin University and teaches part-time at the graduate school of Tokyo Institute of Technology and the Faculty of Law at Waseda University. He obtained his M.A. in TESOL from Columbia University and Ph.D. in Computer Science from the University of Tsukuba. He was a visiting research fellow at the University of Oxford during 1998–1999 and 2007–2008. He has presented many papers at major international conferences such as EUROCALL, GLoCALL, ASIA CALL, WORLD CALL, AACE, AILA, EduLearn, ASIA TEFL, and TESOL. He specializes in educational technology, CALL, TESOL, applied linguistics, and speech recognition. His university e-portfolio can be accessed via the shortcut URL: bit.ly/1QaTwWs.

Takeshi Sato is Associate Professor in the Division of Language and Culture Studies at Tokyo University of Agriculture and Technology, Japan. He holds an M.A. both from Keio University and in TESOL from the Institute of Education which is now part of University College London. His current academic interests are L2 vocabulary acquisition, computer- and mobile-assisted language learning, and pedagogy from English as a Lingua Franca perspective. His articles can be found in the *TESOL Quarterly*, *ReCALL*, *Asian EFL Journal*, *Ampersand*, the *Journal of English as an International Language*, etc. See his publications at Academia.edu: http://tuat.academia.edu/TakeshiSato or at ResearchGate: http://www.researchgate.net/profile/Takeshi_Sato6.

Chapter 1
Introduction: Contextualizing Mobile Language Learning in Japan

Abstract This chapter first introduces the organization of the whole book and its genesis in the collaboration of the authors at an international applied linguistics conference. The first section also touches upon the variety of universities represented, and how the case study chapters follow a similar structure. Next, mobile-assisted language learning (MALL) is defined within e-learning and technology-assisted language learning (TELL) fields by contextualizing MALL into cultural, disciplinary, and historical dimensions. Then the development of MALL in Japan is traced from the mobile Internet, about which little has been published, to the early mobile phone stage and recent smartphone and tablet era, through a literature review. Data on Japanese infant use of handheld devices lastly provide a glimpse of the future.

Organization of This Book

The authors represent three universities in Japan, two in Tokyo and one in Osaka, public and private, large and small, for women and coeducational. Their mobile language learning initiatives arose independently but are brought together in this SpringerBrief to show readers concerned with language teaching how such technologies may be implemented in various contexts. The authors presented together at the International Association of Applied Linguistics AILA World Congress in Brisbane, Australia (Obari et al. 2014). Sato then coordinated the book proposal with Springer Science + Business Media in Singapore, which organized a triple-blind review. The authors are thus delighted to offer this contribution to the international academic community concerned with applying new technologies to language education.

The book is organized around case studies at the three universities. This introduction presents a method to understand a technical concept or academic subfield, mobile-assisted language learning (MALL) in this case, by placing the idea or area of study in its cultural, disciplinary, and temporal contexts. This chapter also elaborates on the historical development of mobile Internet, pioneered in Japan, and

S. McCarty et al., *Implementing Mobile Language Learning Technologies in Japan*, SpringerBriefs in Education, DOI 10.1007/978-981-10-2451-1_1

its applications to language learning. While particular references in this book are often to Japan, the issues are of common concern with language teaching educators in other countries. The historical dimension then leads to Chap. 2, the pedagogical dimension of theory and practical implementation. The sociocultural approach and hypotheses based on previous studies will be reflected and tested in the Chaps. 3, 4 and 5 case studies. Each case study follows a similar outline, first setting the institutional/pedagogical context briefly, then the technological context of infrastructure and portable devices available. Implementation sections detail the specific initiatives with a view to their effectiveness, and each case study chapter concludes with recommendations for other institutions. The concluding Chap. 6 will summarize the history and pedagogy (Chaps. 1, 2), then analyze the diverse cases and how the results as a whole confirm or diverge from previous hypotheses. While each case study emphasizes advice to other practitioners considering the application of mobile technologies to education, the summation of the findings in the concluding chapter also offers practical considerations for future innovations.

Contextualizing and Defining Mobile Language Learning

This section offers a framework for defining mobile-assisted language learning (MALL), by understanding it in its cultural, disciplinary, and temporal contexts. It sheds light on the problem of definitions, which are often circular, insufficient, varying over time, and contradicted by different sources, by helping to distinguish which definition is more accurate, and why. Because, to a great extent, defining is contextualizing, this method can help to define subfields or concepts in their fuller dimensionality. This method has been applied to various fields including EFL and e-learning (McCarty 2005). Japanese and American linguists used a worksheet similar to the grid in Fig. 1.1 to define technical terms and areas of study in their own disciplines (McCarty 2014).

The focus of this book, mobile language learning, provides an example of defining technical terms and practices in their fuller dimensionality. MALL, near the bottom right corner of Fig. 1.1, is contextualized as an instance of technology-enhanced language learning (TELL), the whole lower half of the chart. TELL in turn is a sub-field or application of educational technology, the upper half of the chart, which in the current electronic or digital age is generally termed e-learning.

Above and below MALL in Fig. 1.1 are related manifestations of (TELL), not as abstract concepts but in the historical context in which the practices developed. That order is the temporal dimension, with ubiquitous learning still mostly in the future. Thus the above right section must also be listed in chronological order, which helps to gauge the accuracy of many competing or conflated definitions of the terms: (a) *distance education*, which is still mostly correspondence education in practice around the world, (b) *e-learning*, which has been used most widely to cover all forms of digital learning (including CD-ROMs in CALL labs), and (c) *online*

Field	Institutional / Cultural Context	Disciplinary Context	< past Historical / Temporal Context future >
Educational Technology / e-Learning	❖ Cultural attitudes toward educational technology ❖ Campus IT infrastructure ❖ Learners' ICT skill levels ❖ Computers, media players, hardware available to learners ❖ Mobile Internet, e.g., smart-phones, tablets and e-books ❖ Ubiquitous computing	❖ Correspondence / Distance Education ❖ e-Learning (electronic, actually digital technologies) ❖ Online Education (including blended courses) ❖ m-Learning (mobile) ❖ u-Learning (ubiquitous learning) via sensor networks	
Technology-Enhanced Language Learning (TELL)	❖ Cultural attitudes toward foreign language learning / willingness to communicate ❖ Institutional culture (of the university or school) ❖ Language / Computer Labs ❖ Learners' foreign language levels and individual concerns ❖ Learners' use of their own mobile devices for language learning and communication	❖ Computer-Assisted Instruction (CAI) for language learning ❖ Computer-Assisted Language Learning (CALL) ❖ Network / Internet-Based Language Learning ❖ Mobile-Assisted Language Learning (MALL) ❖ Ubiquitous Language Learning	

Fig. 1.1 Contextualizing mobile language learning

education, which is most recent and relies on the Internet for synchronous and/or asynchronous communication. Online education includes blended learning, because use of the Internet is incorporated into such classes. Online academic conferences (Shimabukuro 2000) for educator development are also a form of online education, which can be hybrid conferences if there is also a physical venue.

Mobile learning and ubiquitous learning, in the same upper right section of Fig. 1.1, moving from the present toward the future, are still forms of the umbrella concept e-learning, and can be used for online education, whether at a distance, in blended courses, informally or in independent study.

The temporal dimension can be verified by examining the development of these practices in academic disciplines, such as by citation or content analysis, which would show, for example, that e-learning is the umbrella concept in the literature of related disciplines. Such definitions are more accurate because one cannot go into the past and substitute an abstraction for how certain disciplines developed. There are technical terms that have different meanings even in different branches of applied linguistics, so a definition cannot be separated from the disciplinary context and its temporal unfolding (the whole right side of Fig. 1.1). The main difference between a field and a discipline in this sense is that a field represents all the possible areas of study, whereas in practice only certain areas are developed, because of various priorities such as the topic of journals, availability of research funds, or the current popularity of certain technologies. A discipline thus consists of the resulting predominant terminology, specialized discourses, a canon of peer-reviewed and cited literature, academic societies, university degree programs, and influential scholars.

The default context of any discussion should be the world, so when it comes to the locations where disciplines and pedagogies are practiced over time, the cultural context also needs to be considered, and within each nation or educational system there are often different institutional cultures. The left side of Fig. 1.1 shows some factors that affect the extent to which the practices on the right side could be implemented effectively. Among those factors, aside from infrastructure and devices available, particularly important for those teaching abroad are cultural attitudes toward the subject matter and toward technology. The uptake and effectiveness of MALL and other pedagogical practices are thus affected by cultural and institutional factors on the left side of Fig. 1.1. Some details of the chart are beyond the scope of this book, but the method offers guidelines both to define a practice and to implement it effectively in a certain place and time.

Keeping this framework in mind, the pedagogical practice of MALL rests upon cultural and institutional factors such as the educational system, the desirability and availability of mobile devices in the local community, and the infrastructure for mobile Internet. In the disciplinary dimension, MALL is an instance of mobile learning, and coexists with other digital or online forms of TELL, particularly as CALL has been reinterpreted by its practitioners to include MALL. Also in the temporal dimension, moving toward the future, ubiquitous learning is connected to MALL insofar as there is a mobile component involved. Ubiquitous computing, applicable to ubiquitous learning and ubiquitous language learning, is discussed later in this chapter. Having contextualized MALL, its technology can be defined more specifically in this section, traced in its development and applications particularly in the case of Japan in the following section, and then mobile pedagogy will be discussed in the next chapter.

Mobile language learning, not in itself but as it has actually developed in practice, can be defined as the formal or informal acquisition to some extent through study or exercise of a second or foreign language, utilizing handheld, portable, or wearable devices for the purpose of language learning. Mobile devices described in case studies in this book include mobile phones and smart phones as well as media players such as the iPod, and tablets such as the iPad. One key line dividing these portable, handheld, digital devices is their Internet connectivity. Media players and mobile phones without Internet access represent an earlier era because of the huge difference in possibilities opened up by the global Internet. The iPod, along with podcasting, which is detailed in Chap. 4, represents an intermediate stage where materials are obtained online but listened to offline. The Web access and apps available to smartphones and tablets now represent a new era that is much more user-friendly and empowering for learners. Thus the MALL that is possible in much of the world today can be characterized as learning languages at any time, in any place, as needed, at the individual learner's own pace, and online, connected both to resources on demand and to other people using the target languages.

Development of Mobile Language Learning in Japan

Mobile Internet

While the Web technically started in 1993, it took some time to develop into a global network. Higher educational institutions in Japan gained domain names and Web servers by 1995, which spurred the evolution from language labs to CALL labs using CAI software locally, then rapidly to Internet-connected computer labs (upper right side of Fig. 1.1).

Japan was one of the pioneering countries in mobile phone technologies, but with a business culture that eschewed free services, so by the end of the 1990s there were a limited number of mobile sites with proprietary access through different protocols of the major telecommunication providers. Bandwidth was limited, and users paid for the time waiting for downloaded content to appear, with subscriber fees from big companies such as Disney. But many organizations wished to have a mobile Web presence to reach customers or viewers for only the cost of using a mobile phone service provider. To make mobile Websites required different software for the format of each major telecom. Screens were tiny, eight Japanese characters or 16 English or ASCII characters across, and photos had to be less than 10 kilobytes to display on typical models. At that time, in the year 2000, McCarty made one of the first educational mobile phone sites, utilizing specifications for compact HTML by NTT Docomo under consideration by the W3 Consortium that manages the Web. The mobile site, with HTML markup done by hand, included bilingual haiku, which was a form of MALL for learners of English or Japanese, a photo, and link to email the author. In a practical English class conducted in a computer lab, students learned used a Web page making program to make their own Web pages from 1999 to 2002, then their own mobile phone sites from 2002 to 2004. In retrospect, it may have been the first classroom application of this kind in the world, showing the potential of MALL by palpably motivating student-generated content (discussed later) to address the outside world in English.

In 2007 the author also established a MALL site using the online service Winksite <http://winksite.com/> (McCarty 2009a; Wang and Heffernan 2009, p. 478). Both the year 2000 site (see Fig. 1.2) and Winksite have a Web view by PC, and the 2000 site also pioneered global access from Web-capable mobile phones.

From Ubiquitous Computing to Ubiquitous Mobile Language Learning

Ubiquitous mobile language learning is the ultimate goal of MALL in the future (thus illustrated at the bottom of the two right side quadrants of Fig. 1.1) where learning is wholly unobstructed and facilitated by the surrounding environment. It can be predicted to become more immersive, less noticed as a deliberate act with a

Fig. 1.2 Mobile Internet site accessible worldwide since 2000 (Web view)

device, and more like a constant and seamless lifestyle. It will continue to be mobile insofar as people have mobility, but it will be operating more and more in the background, invisibly and automatically.

Even the way ubiquitous computing has been defined and practiced so far points toward great changes in the near future. The Internet of Things (IoT), which is the interface between the physical world and cyberspace, has become widely noticed recently as a growing area (Dormehl 2014), yet specialists have been developing its functions for many years. In 1994, Toyota spinoff Denso invented QR code (see Fig. 1.3), a two-dimensional square grid that mobile phone sensors can read and convert to a URL address, connecting the phone to a mobile Website with just a click. It is scalable in size, so that it appears on name cards and big buildings in Tokyo. iPad apps are now available so that the camera function of a tablet computer can read QR code and access the URL it represents. Some mobile phones have used

Fig. 1.3 QR code made in 2006 for mobile phones to access the site in Fig. 2

an alternative system with an infrared sensor. Hospitals have used either a supermarket style bar code or QR code worn like a bracelet on the wrist of patients, through which nurses, holding a scanner connected to a PC, easily and accurately access the electronic chart of patients in the hospital database (McCarty 2011).

Embedded systems, which are software programs built into the environment for specific tasks, handle tasks like controlling appliances while a family is away. In location-based services (see Figs. 1.4 and 1.5), the GPS function in mobile phones alerts users on the go to nearby restaurants and the like, including special offers. Another example researched was to prepare tourist areas of Kyoto so that, in case of a sudden earthquake or other disaster, tourists unfamiliar with the area could point their mobile phones at any sensors on two-dimensional surfaces and be directed to relevant mobile sites (see Fig. 1.4), with maps to the nearest hospital or evacuation route (Hirano et al. 2007).

There are generations of mobile phones, with their capabilities depending on how the devices and infrastructure such as transmission towers are upgraded. In 2006 it was reported that 75 % of Japan's residents used a mobile phone, and the third generation (3G) allowed for interactive TV, telemedicine, GPS, location-based services, stock transactions, and electronic payments that previously required cards with embedded IC chips. GPS could help find lost children or the elderly.

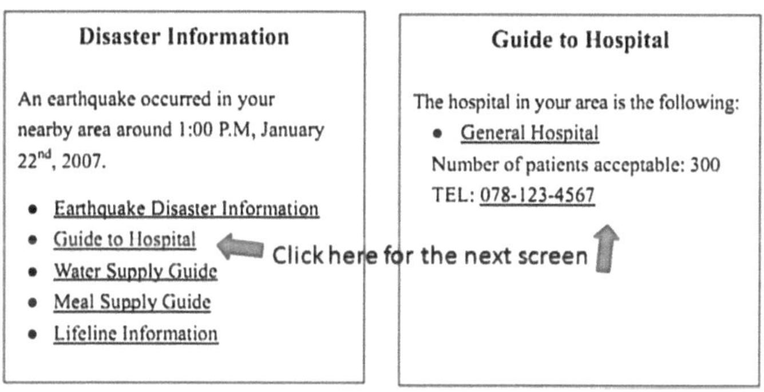

Fig. 1.4 Applying location-based services to public service information

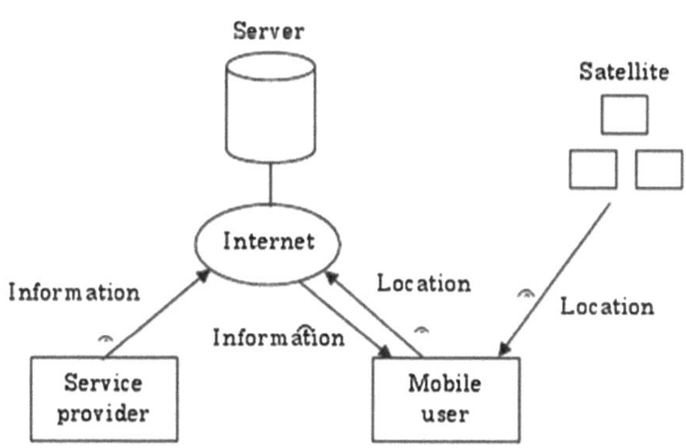

Fig. 1.5 Architecture of location-based services, from Hirano et al. (2007)

Electronic money and ticket applications included credit card functions, vending machine payments, office or building access, and swiping a mobile phone at the gates of rail and subway lines (Asian Technology Information Program 2006).

Thus, in 2014, when Apple announced a mobile payment system, it was ten years after such IC chips were in all Japanese mobile phones. Sony invented the FeliCa chip in 1989, which was first used in Hong Kong subways in 1997, then Japan Railways in 2001, and introduced to Japanese mobile phones in 2004 (AFP/Jiji 2014). Cards or phones do not have to touch the reader but just get close enough to the sensors, which apply fuzzy logic. Student ID cards at Osaka Jogakuin University similarly swipe a reader as part of the attendance management system.

It has long been evident to pioneer researchers that situated u-learning can extend to hybrid or pervasive learning where embedded systems in the urban environment allow mobile phones to access computer networks through codes on flat surfaces or various sensors (Ogata and Yano 2003). In that light, it can be predicted that ubiquitous computing technologies, such as the Internet of things and location-based services, will be applied increasingly to education and to MALL.

Yahya et al. begin to conceptualize the nascent pedagogy of ubiquitous learning (2010), particularly learning just what is needed at a certain time from context-aware systems. Hwang (2014) extends this view, defining smart learning environments pedagogically in terms of context-aware ubiquitous learning. This discussion is still largely at a technological and pan-disciplinary level, not applied yet to language learning. Ubiquitous mobile learning is a futuristic end point, which may best serve to suggest criteria or principles toward best practices when applied to mobile language learning.

Mobile Learning in Japan: Pioneering Initiatives (Circa 2000–2009)

Mobile phones are heavily used throughout Asia (World Bank 2014), but it has often been observed that the ICT culture of Japan has centered on mobile phones more than computers, unlike other developed countries, over the whole span from the 1990s to the present. As a result, foreign teachers tend to think that students lack computing skills, as computers are used formally in schools, while students may be highly skilled in mobile or smartphones that they use privately. A new personal information privacy law in 2005 made it more difficult for teachers to harness the mobile phones of students for class assignments, because teachers do not have the right to know the email address of students' private devices. Some students prefer to separate school work from their personal communication device, although the tide is turning toward more teacher–student contact online through social media (McCarty 2009b, 2010). If students do not all participate voluntarily, it violates a democratic sense of equality in Japanese education. Mobile devices thus present a dilemma to educators and tend to be underutilized for learning. Nevertheless, teachers have experimented over the years with M-learning or MALL, sometimes with successful results, or have worked around the problem by giving all students a mobile platform, incorporated into the curriculum, as detailed in Chap. 4.

MALL initiatives in Japan in this section must be confined to cases whose results were published, and the chronological order is according to the year of publication rather than when the experiments first took place. For example, having students view the bilingual mobile Internet site from the year 2000, as shown above, and having students make mobile phone homepages in the following years, was first reported in McCarty (2009a).

As early as 2002 in Japan, mobile phones were reportedly harnessed for EFL class exercises, by subscribing the students to a mailing list and Web board (Dias 2002). However, at that time the students must have voluntarily paid their own mobile phone service providers for the emails, data downloaded, and time spent browsing online. Before smartphones and tablets, campus and home computers were the main route to browse the Web, and optimization for mobile phones tends to be an afterthought even now. But in Japan's mobile-centered culture, Morita was one of the first to point out that Web-based training (WBT) materials need to be redesigned for mobile phones (2003).

Moving toward using mobile phones more natively, or in view of the small screens at the time, teachers experimented with MALL for EFL and Japanese (JSL) vocabulary (Thornton and Houser 2005; Houser 2007; Maclean and Elwood 2008; Lin et al. 2008), while Houser and Thornton further integrated mobile phones into an early version of the learning management system Moodle (2005). Thornton and Houser found that students did not mind the small screens and had positive attitudes toward M-learning (2005), but student motivation toward MALL, fear or willingness to try new technologies, may differ in other Japanese contexts. Students in other countries may have been deterred by the screen size (Wang and Heffernan 2009, p. 484) if mobile phones were not as central to their daily life as in Japan. Issues of screen size and device preferences will be revisited below, and reflected in the findings of the case studies.

As more and more teachers eyed the mobile phones nearly all students carried as possible learning vehicles, Japan-based Wang and Higgins sounded a cautionary note about the limitations of M-learning at that stage (2006), despite the advent of smartphones (3G). They asserted that M-learning was confined to an auxiliary role for several reasons. "With m-devices, currently mainly mobile phones, PDAs, and iPods, proponents say people can learn … on the move … away from their offices or classrooms" (p. 4), but Wang and Higgins thought that, realistically, the devices were favored for relaxing entertainment or personal communications, so students would lack the motivation for M-learning. Students would use alternatives like dictionaries or computers for actual learning, as habits take time to change. Fears were being raised that overuse of mobile phones could cause health problems such as brain tumors. Among the pedagogical limitations of M-learning, unlike other forms of e-learning, tracking for assessment or timely teacher interactions were more difficult, as students used their mobile devices independently. Issues of any distance education program needed to be faced, such as confirming student identities for tests; the need for self-discipline, which may account for 20–30 % average dropout rates in online courses; or the preference for face-to-face attention over distance communication. Students also faced distractions outside of class, and had to spend money on their mobile Internet access as well as time (2006, pp. 4–6).

Technical limitations included the small screens at the time and low resolution, which could cause eyestrain. The option of directly printing out documents to read was not available to mobile phones. Input was not user-friendly, with different modes and large numbers of double-byte characters in Japanese, less than one-tenth the speed of computer input (Wang and Higgins 2006, pp. 6–7). Internet access was slow and Web pages were not necessarily available in WML for mobile phones at the time, while fonts might not display the foreign languages studied (pp. 7–8). There was a lack of standardization and compatibility among mobile phone models and network transmission formats. While the U.S. was using earlier generation networks, 3G in Japan did not support global roaming. There were drawbacks in using both WiFi for Internet access and Bluetooth for connecting different devices. Mobile phones at the time also lacked memory, limiting the length and functionality of emails (pp. 9–10). Mobile phone use was prohibited in some public places such as hospitals, trains or subways (p. 10), a limitation of mobile learning not solved even now.

After Web 2.0 technologies showed promise for MALL, Wang and Higgins (2008) and Wang and Heffernan (2009) became optimistic about its potential. In any case, the observed limitations of M-learning at the dawn of smartphones can provide hypotheses to examine whether the limitations still persist to some extent or have been overcome.

Continuing in chronological order as per the method established in this chapter, responding to Wang and Higgins (2006), Gromik (2009) had students at Tohoku University in Sendai use their cell phones to make video diaries of 15–30 s per entry to be posted online. He attributed the generally positive reception of the project by students, with some reservations, to the impact of Web 2.0 technologies in "redefining the Internet as a platform for individual content delivery, especially in terms of audio and visual productions" (p. 259). Related topics of podcasting and video blogging or vlogging are detailed later in the Chap. 4 case study.

Wang and Heffernan (2009) examined MALL in light of Web 2.0 and advances in mobile phone technologies. By 2007 there were about 100 million mobile phone contracts, equivalent to nearly 80 % of Japan's population, while China had over 500 million. 3G, begun in 2004, was used by 75 % of subscribers by 2007 (p. 473), which facilitated the gradual change to smartphones.

A Japanese university survey reported in 2007 found that 70 % of respondents used their mobile phones 30-90 min a day, and 63 % would like to use their phones for language learning. Japanese university students carried their mobile phones everywhere, communicating largely through text messages (Wang and Heffernan 2009, p. 474), conducting much of their social life by 2007 at a distance.

Web 2.0, which turned consumers into participants and producers as well, by 2007 featured podcasting, blogs, wikis, social networking sites (SNS), YouTube [more about these technologies in Chap. 4], and the virtual world Second Life, all of which were researched and utilized for language teaching (Wang and Heffernan 2009, p. 475). The idea of Web 2.0 was extended to CALL and Mobile 2.0, which was characterized as a mobile interface to Web 2.0 affordances (pp. 475–476). The advantage of mobile phones over PCs for the same purposes of vocabulary, composition, and so forth, was their mobility, everywhere learners go. Having students submit evaluations by mobile phone was found to be more effective than by PC or on paper in one survey (p. 476). On campus PCs, students needed to sign in, whereas email alerts could be sent to students' mobile phones in real time. Surveys by different researchers in 2005 and 2007 found that all college students had mobile phones, and 99 % used mobile email (p. 477). It was not likely at that point, however, that Mobile 2.0 had overcome all the limitations detailed by Wang and Higgins (2006), not to mention the issue of student participation having to be voluntary, because of the personal information privacy law in effect since 2005.

Wang and Heffernan (2009) recommend the mobile site builder Winksite (discussed above) for blogs, journals, chat forums, and conducting polls. Teachers can post homework, announcements, quizzes, and feedback on previous assignments. The site can be customized for students to read target language sources like magazines and do group work such as writing assignments (p. 478). The most popular social networking sites (SNS) at the time, such as Mixi [founded in 2004, with only a Japanese language interface, detailed in McCarty (2009b)], and blog hosting sites such as Livedoor, were all accessible by mobile phones. Mobile social software, integrated with SNS, allowed for chats with strangers in mobile massive online game environments. Among them were English games as well. Language learners on their own often downloaded software to support watching movies or creating flash cards for vocabulary and grammar study. Short message services (SMS) on mobile phones, integrated with instant messaging (IM), allowed for real-time communications with PC as well as mobile users (pp. 478–479).

The above capabilities of mobile phones, along with other functions such as GPS, in 26 % of mobile phones by 2007, and mobile search (Wang and Heffernan 2009, p. 479) were suggestive of MALL possibilities. After Poodle, by Houser and Thornton (2005), Sapporo Gakuin University provided only feedback and quiz modules to mobile phones (Wang and Heffernan 2009, p. 481) among the many Moodle LMS functions available to computers. Suggestions are offered for setting up mobile sites and using QR code to direct mobile phones to their URL (Wang and Heffernan 2009, pp. 481–482; see also McCarty 2009a). MALL initiatives in other countries start to appear in the literature in Japan during this period, but not enough to compare the relative development of technology and pedagogy, which would go beyond the scope of this chapter in any case.

MALL in Japan: Smartphone and Tablet Era (Circa 2010-Present)

After the pioneering initiatives described above, the growing interest of teachers in harnessing devices inseparable from students, combined with greater capabilities of smartphones and new types of mobile devices such as tablet computers, led to a vast increase in MALL experiments and published studies.

Space does not allow full coverage here, but Burston summarizes hundreds of MALL studies while finding only a tiny percentage that scientifically demonstrate positive learning outcomes of MALL implementations in higher education (2013, 2014). His summaries span 20 years and cover many studies based in Japan, some similar to the previous section of this chapter, and others after the advent of smartphones and tablets. Among the latter since 2010, the largest number of implementations still aims for target language vocabulary acquisition. Mobile phones have been harnessed for extensive or graded reading, and connected to the campus IT infrastructure for monitoring or tracking. Mobile Website builders and sites for text-based L2 interactions have been employed. Pronunciation apps have been developed, and listening exercises on the Web have been assigned. Mobile devices used for MALL included the iPod Touch, clickers for instant polling, or audience response software installed in students' mobile phones. For fuller details, Burston (2013) is available at the URL in the References section of this book.

Japan's telecommunications infrastructure has remained near the cutting edge in fast broadband and so forth, after private carriers pioneered proprietary mobile networks. To this day, though, Japan's technologies work well nationally but have not become a global standard exported and localized abroad. Nevertheless, in a presentation to the International Telecommunication Union, Morita (2006) of the former national telecommunications carrier NTT outlined the government's u-Japan Plan for nationwide optical fiber networks, to be seamlessly integrated with the Internet and mobile networks by 2010. The "u" stands for ubiquitous, which remains a goal along with the interoperability or convergence of fixed and mobile networks in the national infrastructure.

Although the iPhone first appeared in 2007, the iPhone 3G was introduced into Japan in 2008, breaking with its popularity the barrier foreign goods have often faced in Japan. The iPhone was not the first smartphone, but it was fashionable, user-friendly, and increasingly useful as app developers focused on it. The screen size was larger than most previous mobile phones; Websites with markup for PCs could be displayed, and sections could be enlarged by touch.

The Google Android mobile OS is even more widely used than the iOS, not only in the number of installations, with over a billion users, but also in the types of appliances it runs: touch screen devices such as smartphones and tablets, TVs, cars, watches, game consoles, digital cameras, and other electronics (Wikipedia 2016). Wearable devices with connectivity such as the Apple Watch and Google Glass have entered the market as well, but their affordability and practicality for formal learning will be an issue for future iterations of wearable technology.

For pleasure reading, self-study or educational purposes, handheld offline readers for e-books have found a niche, with a larger screen size than mobile phones, lighter than books, and with improved readability over most computer fonts. This book, however, emphasizes that the power of mobility lies to a great extent in what can be accessed remotely, so online functionality has become a defining characteristic of mobile use for pleasure or learning. In this sense, a greater change was the advent of tablet computers, particularly the iPad in 2010, for viewing Web pages and so forth nearly like PCs, but wireless, mobile, and online when within range of WiFi coverage. The iPhone and iPad ran on the same operating system iOS and used similar software, but, salient for mobile learning, the iPad could accommodate e-books and other apps that benefited from more screen space. Using the iPad for MALL from 2012 to 2015 is detailed in Chap. 4.

One study in Japan examined university class study of electronic handouts on the 25 × 19 cm iPad 2 compared with the 20 × 13.5 cm iPad Mini, which was 23 % thinner and 53 % lighter. The main difference was thought to be the screen size (Runnels and Rutson-Griffiths 2013, p. 278), but the weight may also have been a key factor. EFL lecturers clearly preferred the iPad 2, while students showed no preference on typing and overall satisfaction. For ease of use, students slightly preferred the iPad Mini. While students preferred the iPad 2 for use in class, 78 % preferred the iPad Mini for use at home. Teachers' comments focused on screen size, finding the iPad Mini difficult to operate and too small to see whole pages at once. Students and administrators, however, believed the iPad Mini was easier to use everywhere outside of class, because it was easier to carry around. The contrasting views of EFL lecturers and their students were interpreted as reflecting prior experiences with mobile devices, more familiarity of teachers with devices like the iPad 2, whereas students accustomed to using smartphones did not find the smaller iPad Mini screen an issue. Later the authors added that the overall smaller size and weight of the iPad Mini was an advantage for students. PDF format classroom handouts, being originally designed for paper, might be part of the problem, they concluded (pp. 280–282). Indeed, using new technologies like the iPad natively, with new formats based on apps such as iBooks for the iPad, would allow for more user-friendly activities and interactivity (see Chap. 4 for more discussion of usability issues).

Byrne and Diem (2014) provide data comparing mobile English language learners in different countries, which could contribute to hypotheses as to whether or not EFL learners of university age in Japan have distinct characteristics because of the predominance of mobile phones throughout their lives. Byrne and Diem embedded a survey in a popular English grammar app for the Android platform, reaching 3759 respondents in an authentic and voluntary context (2014, pp. 3–4). They note that smartphones and tablets can personalize learning by tracking user profiles and environmental parameters, particularly through GPS and apps that interact seamlessly with the campus learning management system. Teachers could get involved in student choices of apps that many are already selecting to support their university studies. Students reportedly used mobile dictionaries, translators, flash cards, and vocabulary games most often on their own. They found mobile apps easy to understand, flexible and convenient, as they could practice their target languages anytime and anywhere. University faculty or staff could recommend or build apps, keeping in mind student preferences for social contact, audio, video, and short texts (pp. 5–6).

Among the results reported by Byrne and Diem, Japanese native speaking respondents were only 1.37 % of active users of the grammar app, or 100 among

$N = 2214$. The native languages were French and Spanish, 26 % each; Italian and Russian, 10 % each; German, 9 %; Korean, 7 %; Japanese, 5 %; and Thai, 3 %. Males totaled 56 % (64 % of Japanese), and nearly 50 % (44 % of Japanese) were under age 25. Most regarded their English CEFR level as beginner (64 %) or elementary (12 %). The results suggest that apps should be targeted to those levels, with separate apps possibly appealing to the interests of adolescent females and older males. Since it was a demographic study, only inferences could be drawn about possible cultural factors behind the comparatively low response rates of Asians (2014, pp. 8–15). Thus while the Japanese differed from Europeans and Russians in responsiveness to the survey, they were typical of Asians in this respect. This may show that there is great potential scope for Japanese and other students to engage in autonomous mobile language learning, utilizing apps at suitable levels that foster interactivity.

White and Mills (2014) examined the attitudes of Japanese university EFL students toward using mobile phones for their classes, first citing various studies. As of 2012, 95.6 % of the public used mobile phones, while by 2008 mobile phones were the preferred device for young people to access the Internet. Smartphones alleviated many of the limitations of M-learning found in earlier studies. Students used their mobile phones to enhance learning, particularly by photographing the class whiteboard or other sources of information, recording lectures, and accessing L2 vocabulary learning apps. Students also used English news apps for reading and listening to videos on the Web (pp. 1–3). Different researchers found conflicting results as to whether students preferred to use mobile phones or PCs (p. 4), so attitudes may differ according to factors such as the cognitive load of the assignment.

One Japanese university group yielded positive results among 88 first year students by promoting self-directed learning with Nintendo DS gaming devices to improve TOEIC reading scores, but a later study after the class testing seemed to show that their motivation had been temporary or instrumental. A university group found that using the iPad enhanced group interactions, with 16 of 34 university students finding it useful, while 7 did not, preferring to use PCs. A junior high school study found positive effects of the iPad on confidence, anxiety reduction, and willingness to communicate in English, particularly among Japanese boys (White and Mills 2014, pp. 4–5).

Among the results of their own studies, White and Mills found that in 2011, 99.5 % of 403 students owned mobile phones, reaching 100 % of 162 respondents in 2012. Among those devices, smartphones were 54 % in 2011, but 85 % in 2012. In both years the smartphone operating systems were about half Android and half iOS. Only 6 % of students in 2011 and 7 % in 2012 used apps explicitly dedicated to language learning, though use of dictionary functions rose from 11 % in 2011 to 21 % in 2012 (2014, pp. 7–9).

From 2011 to 2012, student attitudes toward MALL changed from harmful or not helpful, 4–3 %; neutral, 29–19 %; and helpful or very helpful, 67–78 %. Over just that one year, many students had changed to different devices or apps available to smartphones, and the authors expected that at least the students who thought

MALL would be very helpful for EFL studies, from 24 % in 2011 to 35 % in 2012, would also be receptive to using their mobile phones for explicitly educational purposes. Ritsumeikan University students used mobile phones mainly for entertainment and personal communication as of 2012 (White and Mills 2014, pp. 9–11), using dictionary apps and the like independently, as they had not yet experienced MALL being assigned in classes or integrated into the curriculum. However, mobile technology use is evolving rapidly among students, and teachers.

A survey taken in 2013 in the Tokyo metropolitan area provides a view of mobile phone culture in Japan as it is emerging between parents and small children. Benesse Educational Research and Development Institute (2014) examined media use and awareness among parents, who found mobile phones indispensable, and how the devices had penetrated the daily lives of children. 3234 mothers with firstborn children 6 months to 6 years old responded to the mailed questionnaire. Results showed 60 % of mothers overall using smartphones, including 80.2 % of those under 30. 22.1 % of 2-year-olds in such families were exposed to smartphones almost every day, 21.6 % of 3-year-olds, and more than 10 % for ages 1 and 4-6, while only 4 % of babies 6–12 months old had daily exposure. Overall, a majority of small children were exposed to smartphones at least rarely. More than 30 % of such parents overall set rules for mobile use, fewer than for TV watching. Parents showed awareness of possible pros and cons of mobile use. It enriches knowledge (81.5 %), children can enjoy singing and dancing (77.1 %), and it develops self-expression through crafts and drawing (68.7 %), whereas parents were concerned that smartphones are bad for eyes or health (86 %) and addictive (74.6 %).

By comparison, in the U.S., "children younger than 2 years old watch nearly an hour of television a day and almost 40 percent have used a smartphone or other mobile device" (Calvert 2014), rising to 80 % for children aged 2–4. The amount and quality of screen time has thus become a global issue.

Although the Benesse survey involved generations before and after university age, having been conducted in Japanese and reported in English (2014), it offers a glimpse into a future of native mobile users, taking portable media devices for granted as part of their daily environment, before they even enter classrooms with teachers who may or may not be prepared to reach such learners.

References

AFP/Jiji. (2014, September 14). Apple a decade behind Japan's mobile payment curve. *The Japan Times*.

Asian Technology Information Program. (2006). *3G mobile phones in Japan. GLOCOM Global Communications Platform*. Tokyo: International University of Japan. Retrieved from http://www.glocom.org/tech_reviews/tech_report/20061222_atip_s80/

Benesse Educational Research and Development Institute. (2014). *Survey of media use by children and parents*. Tokyo: Child Research Net. Retrieved from http://www.childresearch.net/data/digital/2014_02.html

Burston, J. (2013). Mobile-assisted language learning: A selected annotated bibliography of implementation studies 1994–2012. *Language Learning & Technology, 17*(3),157–224. Retrieved from http://llt.msu.edu/issues/october2013/burston.pdf

Burston, J. (2014). The reality of MALL: Still on the fringes. *CALICO Journal, 31*(1), 103–125.

Byrne, J., & Diem, R. (2014). Profiling mobile English language learners. *JALT CALL Journal, 10* (1), 3–19.

Calvert, K. (2014, October 30). For toddlers it's the quality of screen time that matters, study reveals. *PBS Newshour*. Retrieved from http://www.pbs.org/newshour/rundown/screen-time-toddlers-parents-dont-feel-guilty/

Dias, J. (2002). Cell phones in the classroom: boon or bane? *C@lling Japan, 10*(2), 16–21.

Dormehl, L. (2014, June 8). Internet of things: It's all coming together for a tech revolution. *The Guardian*. Retrieved from http://www.theguardian.com/technology/2014/jun/08/internet-of-things-coming-together-tech-revolution

Gromik, N. (2009). Producing cell phone video diaries. In M. Thomas (Ed.), *Handbook of research on Web 2.0 and second language learning* (pp. 259–273). Hershey, PA: IGI Global.

Hirano, K., Nakatani, Y., McCarty, S., & Masuda, H. (2007). Applications of mobile research in Japan. *Ubiquity, 8*(38), 1–34. New York: Association for Computing Machinery (ACM).

Houser, C. (2007, March 24). Using mobile phones in foreign language education. A presentation at Wireless Ready 1: Podcasting Education and Mobile Assisted Language Learning. Nagoya: NUCB Graduate School.

Houser, C., & Thornton, P. (2005). Poodle: A course management system for mobile phones. *Proceedings of the Third IEEE Workshop on Wireless Technologies in Education* (pp. 159–163). IEEE Computer Society.

Hwang, G.-J. (2014). Definition, framework and research issues of smart learning environments – a context-aware ubiquitous learning perspective. *Smart Learning Environments, 1*(4). Retrieved from http://www.slejournal.com/content/1/1/4

Lin, N., Kajita, S., & Mase, K. (2008). Mobile user behavior and attitudes during story-based kanji learning. *JALT CALL Journal, 4*(1), 3–18.

Maclean, G., & Elwood, J. (2008, May 31). Anytime-anywhere: Mobile phone applications for modern foreign language instruction. A presentation at JALTCALL 2008. Nisshin, Aichi: Nagoya University of Commerce and Business.

McCarty, S. (2005). *Cultural, disciplinary, and temporal contexts of e-learning and English as a foreign language*. Research Papers. *eLearn Magazine*, April 2005 issue. Retrieved from http://elearnmag.acm.org/archive.cfm?aid=1070950

McCarty, S. (2009a). Making mobile phone Websites. In M. Thomas (Ed.), *New frontiers in CALL: Negotiating diversity* (pp. 65–70). Tokyo: JALT CALL SIG.

McCarty, S. (2009b). Social networking behind student lines in Japan. In M. Thomas (Ed.), *Handbook of research on Web 2.0 and second language learning* (pp. 181–201). Hershey, PA: IGI Global.

McCarty, S. (2011). *Ubiquitous computing and online collaboration for open education*. Kuantan, Malaysia: A keynote address at the 5th International Malaysian Educational Technology Convention.

McCarty, S. (2014, July 20). *A multidimensional approach to definitions, applied to e-learning in language education*. Suita, Osaka, Japan: A presentation at the Minpaku Linguistics Circle, National Museum of Ethnology.

McCarty, S. (2010). Social media to motivate language learners from before admission to after graduation. In W. M. Chan, et al. (Eds.), *Media in foreign language teaching and learning* (pp. 87–105). Centre for Language Studies: National University of Singapore.

Morita, M. (2003). Mobile based learning (MBL) in Japan. In *Proceedings of the First Conference on Creating, Connecting and Collaborating through Computing*. IEEE Computer Society.

Morita, N. (2006). *An introduction to NTT's NGN [Next Generation Networks] and new services in Japan. A presentation at the International Telecommunication Union ITU-T/ITU-D Workshop on Standardization and Development of Next Generation Networks.* Dar es Salaam, Tanzania, 3–5 Oct 2006.

Obari, H., Sato, T., Lambacher, S., Nozawa, N., & McCarty, S. (2014, August 11). *Utilizing emerging technologies and social media to enhance EFL learning*. A symposium at the International Association of Applied Linguistics AILA World Congress 2014. Brisbane Convention and Exhibition Centre, Australia.

Ogata, H. & Yano, Y. (2003). *How ubiquitous computing can support language learning*. Tokushima University.

Runnels, J., & Rutson-Griffiths, A. (2013). Tablet PCs in a paperless classroom: Student and teacher perceptions on screen size. *JALT CALL Journal, 9*(3), 275–285.

Shimabukuro, J. (2000). What is an online conference? *The Technology Source*. Retrieved from http://technologysource.org/article/what_is_an_online_conference/

Thornton, P., & Houser, C. (2005). Using mobile phones in English education in Japan. *Journal of Computer Assisted Learning*, *21*(3), 217–228.

Wang, S., & Heffernan, N. (2009). *Mobile 2.0 and mobile language learning*. In M. Thomas (Ed.), *Handbook of research on Web 2.0 and second language learning* (pp. 472–490). Hershey, PA: IGI Global.

Wang, S., & Higgins, M. (2006). Limitations of mobile phone learning. *The JALT CALL Journal, 2*(1), 3–14.

Wang, S., & Higgins, M. (2008). Mobile 2.0 Leads to a Transformation in mLearning. In J. Fong, R. Kwan., & F. L. Wang (Eds.), *Hybrid learning and education conference proceedings* (pp. 225–237). Berlin, Germany: Springer.

White, J., & Mills, D. (2014). Examining attitudes towards and usage of smartphone technology among Japanese university students studying EFL. *CALL-EJ, 15*(2), 1–15.

Wikipedia. (2016). *Android (operating system)*. Retrieved from http://en.wikipedia.org/wiki/Android_(operating_system)

World Bank (2014). *Mobile cellular subscriptions (per 100 people)*. Indicators. The Data Catalog. Retrieved from http://data.worldbank.org/indicator/

Yahya, S., Ahmad, E. A., & Jalil, K. A. (2010). The definition and characteristics of ubiquitous learning: A discussion. *International Journal of Education and Development using Information and Communication Technology (IJEDICT), 6*(1), 117–127.

Chapter 2
Mobile Language Learning Pedagogy: A Sociocultural Perspective

Abstract This chapter provides a theoretical framework for mobile language learning from a sociocultural perspective. While the advantages of personal computers over previous modes have been discussed in terms of e-learning, m-learning with mobile devices opens up new horizons that can enhance user-centered learning. Characteristics of mobile devices such as ownership and mobility can help to personalize language learning. For instance, generating target language contents from learners' life-worlds can help to develop the autonomy and agency required for effective learning in this era of new technology. This chapter reviews the literature important for mobile language learning with the aim of applying the theoretical framework to pedagogies in local settings as seen in the following chapters.

Introduction

This chapter examines the potential impact of mobile technologies on L2 teaching and learning, particularly from a sociocultural perspective. It emphasizes how the *mobility of the connected learner* can allow for transformative pedagogical approaches as compared with the fixity of computer-based L2 learning. Although this book accepts the shorthand usage of 'MALL' in the disciplinary development of technology-enhanced language learning (TELL), as discussed in Chap. 1, the emphasis in CALL and MALL appears to be on the technologies that assist learning, whereas 'mobile language learning' is closer to emphasizing the mobility of the learner when freed from the constraints of fixed places and times. With regular classrooms, computer labs, or home computers, the flow is toward a fixed location before learning can take place, whereas with Internet-connected mobile devices, the flow can be *through* learning experiences, more fully and immersively, closer to ubiquitous learning (Fig. 2.1).

S. McCarty et al., *Implementing Mobile Language Learning Technologies in Japan*, SpringerBriefs in Education, DOI 10.1007/978-981-10-2451-1_2

Fig. 2.1 The ancient Greeks already used (wax) tablets for education. This figure can thus symbolize mobile pedagogy. (Creative Commons attribution: Photo of Greek art about 500 BC by Douris, by Pottery Fan, 2009, CC BY-SA 3.0)

L2 Learning with Mobile Devices Compared with Personal Computers

Computer-based L2 learning began from a paradigm where fixed contents to be acquired were displayed, and interaction took place in terms of the contents, such as through questions about the material with fixed answers. The learner's role was to access the contents and receive knowledge displayed on the computer screen, then answering the questions generated by computer programs. Kozulin (2003) criticizes this predominant paradigm whereby learners are regarded as containers which should be filled with the knowledge and skills transmitted by their teachers.

Recently, however, mobile devices allow for a broader paradigm, including collaboration with peers, with few restrictions of place or time, incorporating resources from personal experiences, and learning can take place through sharing and discussing the resources all participants bring into a community. Learners can now go beyond classroom-based groups and form mobile communities where they find out things on the go and share their unique contributions with the group through the exchange of messages, questions, comments, with attached files of longer text or media such as photos or videos. That is, Internet-connected mobile devices can serve as a tool to enable and develop online learning communities.

MALL, first of all, has structural differences from CALL, whereby L2 learning was conducted with desktop or laptop PCs inside classrooms or, by extension, elsewhere. Pachler et al. (2010) argue that laptop computers cannot be thought of as mobile devices. In CAI or CALL laboratories, target contents tend to be as fixed as the facilities, with students working in isolation even while sitting in close proximity to their peers. The physical setting in effect if not intention influences the learning paradigm. The L2 study materials tend to be prepared as computer software or teacher-selected Internet Websites in which target knowledge and skills happen to be approximated. Thus the move from CAI to CALL and beyond has been subject to both the devices available at the time, including CD-ROMs at one stage, and the evolution of Web functionality from simple read-write functions to so-called Web 2.0 and social media. At the beginning of this book Fig. 1.1 illustrated the evolution from past toward future forms of technology-enhanced language learning.

In different countries around the world, however, it is not a bygone practice for learners to be assigned certain tasks using PCs, answering questions or filling in blanks, for instance, with the aim of acquiring fixed knowledge and skills through the materials accessed. CALL technology was taken up in the first place because it offered new approaches that could not be carried out by traditional materials such as books. Computers were seen as a more efficient tool to accomplish unchanged purposes of displaying certain L2 target items or demonstrating skills for students to practice. There is still a tendency for online pedagogical practices to simulate the former classroom paradigm rather than change to a paradigm better suited to the affordances of new media. Despite tasks and contents being presented with new technology, surpassing the possibilities of traditional media like paper-based books, learners might still be reluctant to take full advantage of such materials, mainly because they would get bored doing the tasks alone. It may therefore be no coincidence that pedagogical concerns for learner autonomy, collaboration, and other sociocultural approaches are coming to the fore contemporaneously with the social Web and mobile technologies.

Mobile learning affords the possibility of different styles of learning, as will be seen later in this chapter and in the case studies. First of all, it is not only devices such as computers but also learners themselves that can generate learning contents. Since learners tend to carry their mobile devices always and wherever they go, any kinds of resources such as texts, links, photos, movies, or sound files that they encounter, record or edit, inside or outside of their classrooms, could be utilized as learning resources by uploading them to sites where they connect with others online. Such resources that each learner finds to be of interest would then be shared socially, discussed with other learners, and exploited for L2 acquisition. Such a process is termed *learner-generated context* (Pachler et al. 2010), which is a conceptual expansion of the also very applicable notion of *learner-generated content* (cf. Lee and McLoughlin 2007). In that respect, mobile technologies can offer a platform for communication that is motivating, and where autonomy and collaboration are mutually reinforcing.

The next chapter will present a case in point, utilizing mobile phone group chats, but first the discussion of pedagogy will be grounded in the situation in Japan, briefly illustrating the educational problems for which mobile technologies and sociocultural approaches may offer needed solutions.

Challenges of Learning English as a Foreign Language in Asian Settings

Learning and teaching English as a foreign language (EFL) tends to be challenging in most Asian countries. This is mainly because such EFL countries offer very limited exposure to English not only in daily lives but also in institutions. In Taiwan, for example, the time to use English is limited in language classrooms for most vocational high school students. They have only two to four hours of English classes a week (Lu 2008). Iranian university students also tend to be exposed to English for a limited time: only once a week for 90 min (Derakhshan and Khodabakhshzadeh 2011). In Thailand, as there are few opportunities to use English in their daily settings, the English language competence of Thai learners, as measured by the national tests such as Ordinary National Educational Test and General Aptitude Test, or by the standardized language proficiency tests such as TOEFL® and TOEIC®, is far from satisfactory, according to Khamkhien (2012).

Learning and teaching English as a foreign language in Japan is also challenging in some ways (Shirai 2011). First of all, there are generally few opportunities to use English authentically in daily life. By definition, in an EFL rather than ESL setting, there is no widespread English speech community or domain of daily life where English is necessary. Thus Japanese people generally do not see a need to master English for their daily purposes. Although the potential opportunities to read text and write messages in English have vastly increased with the advent of ICT such as the Web, email and SNS, English is still not widely perceived as an indispensable skill set, especially in terms of listening and speaking.

Second, related to the first factor, motivation for Japanese people to learn English tends to be low, because it does not stem from daily necessity or societal consensus. Shirai (2011) points out that the primary motivator for college students, for example, is to get higher scores in English language proficiency tests such as the TOEIC® test, in order to demonstrate higher L2 competence to companies or other institutions where such scores are linked to career employment or promotion.

Third, as getting higher scores in proficiency tests tends to be a primary motivator, L2 learning seems to be thought of as information acquisition. Learners tend to expect their teachers to provide L2 knowledge such as vocabulary and grammar, and then they try to possess such items, memorizing their meanings and functions, which passes for successful learning on paper tests. The efforts of such students are thus directed toward understanding texts and copying what teachers write on the blackboard, quietly and passively. It is observed that they seldom answer questions voluntarily, and respond only when asked by the teacher (Tanaka 2009). In this respect, the teaching and learning style can be regarded as receptive (Kubota 2002), teacher-fronted or teacher-centered (Tanaka 2009).

In addition, learning tasks and materials are often decontextualized and bear little relation to students' own life-worlds. English is therefore regarded as something they might need for their future, but of hardly any relevance to their present life-worlds. The resources or texts made in Anglophone countries, as Brown (1990) points out, tend to deal with topics such as international travel and hotels as contexts with English representing a new cosmopolitanism. Yet this kind of content from Anglophone countries might pay insufficient attention to the indigenous contexts in which the texts or resources are used. In sum, among the challenges are the lack of English speech communities, attitudes of teaching and learning as information transmission and acquisition, and decontextualized resources, irrelevant to students' life-worlds, which do not ignite learners' motivation to master English. To tackle such challenges facing English education in Japan and other foreign language situations, the next sections will illustrate pedagogical principles and practices that could bring about more effective L2 learning.

What Is Effective Learning?

Sharples et al. (2005) derive definitions of effective learning from the 1999 US National Research Council recommendations for learner-centered, knowledge-centered, assessment-centered, and community-centered learning. Based on these definitions, Sharples et al. (2005) suggest that learning be a process within the community whereby learners are actively engaged with peers in order to acquire knowledge and skills. Through such a process in communities of practice (Lave and Wenger 1991), which refer to "groups of people who share a concern or a passion for something they do and learn how to do it better as they interact regularly" (Wenger 2011, p. 1), learners could use the resources from their own life-worlds to bring about the contextualization of the target knowledge and skills. To tackle challenges in foreign language settings such as teaching and learning English in Japan, this book proposes that mobile language learning could facilitate effective learning as defined above.

Advantages of Mobile Learning

The advantages of mobile-based L2 learning tend to be discussed in terms of the technology; that is, technologically advanced devices and functions, accessibility of learning resources that can be obtained anytime and anywhere, and the use of various applications for studying. These technological aspects tend to be stressed in examining the effectiveness of mobile learning. Learners have adopted mobile technological affordances more readily than those of personal computers, because mobile devices have already become such requisite tools for life daily in many countries that students have their own smartphones or other mobile devices.

This chapter, however, pays more attention to sociocultural aspects of mobile learning than technological ones. In this view, L2 learners with mobile devices have the advantage of interacting with peers anytime and anywhere with the resources they bring from their own everyday life-worlds (Schutz and Luckmann 1973), which can make their L2 learning more contextualized and effective.

Pachler et al. (2010) show that mobile devices have become indispensable tools for daily life because of their portability, the convergence of technologies, and the decreasing cost for the devices and services. Kukulska-Hulme (2009) also points out three advantages of mobile learning: ownership, mobility, and convergence of technologies.

According to a Japan Ministry of Internal Affairs and Communications report on Internet literacy (2015), 88.1 % of high school students had their own smartphone while 52.2 % of them had their own PC (down from 66.7 % owning a PC the year before), and 80 % of them connected to the Internet more from their smartphone than from personal computers. Likewise, the result of questionnaire research about the use of the Internet conducted by Just System, an IT company in Japan, illustrates that Japanese teenagers are more likely to connect to the Internet via smartphones (n = 116.2) than with personal computers (n = 88.2) (FastAsk 2014). Furthermore, according to a 2012 survey by Kindai University, one of the biggest private universities in Japan, all students of the university owned mobile devices. 94 % of them had smartphones, 21 % had other mobile phones (feature phones), and 7 % had tablets (Kindai University 2013). The report pointed out that all students had at least one mobile device, and some had multiple mobile devices. The ratio of smartphones is increasing, and there will be a demand for more powerful portable devices and functions that are developed to help people stay connected with other people.

Such a trend is seen throughout Asia. For example, the leading index to measure the progress of ICT infrastructure, opportunities, and utilization shows eight Asian countries ranked among the top 25: Australia, Hong Kong, Japan, Macao, New Zealand, Singapore, South Korea, and Taiwan (So 2012). By 2004 there were countries where the diffusion rate of mobile phones reached more than 100 % (Lu 2008; for more recent and detailed data see World Bank 2014).

The popularity of mobile devices could accrue to their use for academic purposes. Stockwell and Hubbard (2013) point out that the familiarity of the use of mobile devices could smoothly transfer technological practices for personal uses into those for institutional uses. For example, the following everyday activities of mobile device users can also serve the purposes of learning: sending and receiving messages, taking photos, attaching files, utilizing social networking services, and so on.

Mobility is a crucial tenet of mobile learning, although its full implications have yet to be realized. It can add a new and personal dimension to the learning and teaching environment in the traditional classroom, while expanding the locus of learning beyond the classroom. To Laurillard, "the mobility of digital technologies creates intriguing opportunities for new forms of learning" (2007, p. 153). More specifics need to be filled in, with more focus on the implications of the mobility of the learner. But to follow up on the opportunities alluded to by Laurillard would imply a radical institutional change in ways of thinking and practices. What would be impossible in the traditional classroom-based learning environment would have to be seen as desirable and subject to experimentation, that is, innovation with all the risks of attempting new pedagogical and technological practices. But it is evident already that learners with their own devices can do such things as to access learning resources and send their feedback or assignments to instructors anytime and anywhere they are. The question is whether students will be left to their own devices or mobile learning will be incorporated into the school philosophy and curriculum.

As in computer-assisted language learning, the representation of L2 with various types of media is also one of the advantages of learning with mobile devices. Many studies support the hypothesis that the convergence of media facilitates learning more effectively than simply written or verbal information. As computers do, contemporary mobile devices can also display any kind of content with several media on one screen (Chun and Plass 1996; Laufer and Hill 2000; Laufer and Hulstijn 2001; Lomicka 1998; Yoshii and Fraitz 2001; Sato and Suzuki 2010, 2012; Sato et al. 2013; Yeh and Wang 2003). Then, of course, insofar as mobile devices are online, their users are connected to a whole world of information and people.

Such onscreen presentation can make lexical items and their linguistic features more salient (Pachler 2001), which is one of the conditions hypothesized for an ideal environment of L2 acquisition (Chapelle 1998), and could therefore lead to more effective learning. Chun and Plass (1996), for example, show that incidental L2 vocabulary acquisition is more effectively enhanced by the combination of text and picture or video glosses along with a reading text than text only. Yoshii and Fraitz (2002) also show that L2 vocabulary learning could be more effectively conducted with a combination of text and picture glosses than with text-only or picture-only glosses.

Moreover, Yeh and Wang (2003) show that a combination of text and picture (or also sound) are more effective glosses than text only. These studies support the hypothesis of a learning advantage in the convergence of media, concluding that multimedia environments, by displaying information in several modes simultaneously, can have positive effects on L2 learning. Compared with displaying target content in fewer dimensions, fuller dimensionality and contextualization can lead to greater understanding. Furthermore, the implementation of technologically advanced functions could enhance L2 learning. Al-Seghayer (2001), for example, shows that animation is a more effective technique than the use of still images for L2 vocabulary learning. Sato et al. (2013) show that time-controlling functions of a mobile-based vocabulary learning application facilitate not only quicker recall of target vocabulary but also more accurate comprehension of the text in which the target vocabulary is embedded.

Despite the fact that MALL also entails disadvantages such as smaller size of screen and the difficulty of inputting texts (Stockwell and Hubbard 2013), not to mention the cost of the device and continuing provider fees, m-learning has been gaining wider recognition, resulting in continuous development and sales of many L2 learning applications for mobile devices in the iTunes Store and Google Play, for reasonable prices or sometimes for free. Mostly unbeknownst to teachers, such applications for L2 study support on mobile devices are being used independently for learning, and sometimes surreptitiously for school assignments, unconstrained by place or time, events or schedules.

As mentioned above, mobile devices allow for more fully dimensional ways of knowledge representation, leading to longer retention or quicker recall of target content, for example. These advantages, however, have been mostly investigated according to an acquisition metaphor (Sfard 1998), which represents only one, quantitative aspect of learning, in terms of which learning is regarded as an activity to acquire things provided by others such as teachers. Other aspects including qualitative, social, and creative dimensions need to be explored for a fuller picture of pedagogy in m-learning as elsewhere.

New Approaches to L2 Learning

The acquisition metaphor or information transmission model may represent one aspect of formal education that is difficult to entirely replace in a structure where teachers conduct activities with expertly selected target content to be practiced and acquired. New mobile technology, however, offers alternative approaches to the learning process itself. Sharples et al. (2007) show how new technology available on mobile devices can change the way learning takes place. Figure 2.2 shows some salient characteristics of learning with technology as recently conceived, evidently influenced by sociocultural pedagogy as well as possibilities opened up by mobile technologies with a view to ubiquitous learning.

One chart cannot capture all the possible nuances, however. Kukulska-Hulme (2009) describes subtle new ways of learning with mobile devices as "continuity or spontaneity of access and interaction across different contexts of use" (p. 273).

Laurillard (2002, 2007) conceptualizes the process of learning with a focus on the interaction between the learner and a partner such as a teacher or other learner. This learning model is called the Conversational Framework, and it defines the

New Learning	New Technology
Personalized	Personal
Learner centered	User centered
Situated	Mobile
Collaborative	Networked
Ubiquitous	Ubiquitous
Lifelong	Durable

Fig. 2.2 Relationship between new learning approaches and new applications of technology (adapted from The Sage Handbook of Elearning Research, A Theory of Learning for the Mobile Age, 2007, p. 223, Table 1. Mike Sharples, Josie Taylor & Giasemi Vavoula)

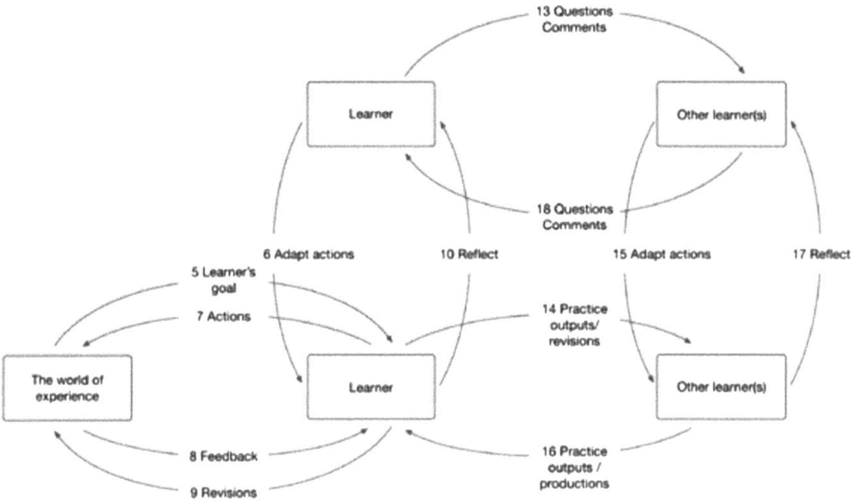

Fig. 2.3 Conversational framework (Reprinted with permission from Diana Laurillard. Mobile Learning: Towards a research agenda, Pedagogical forms for mobile learning: framing research questions, 2007, p. 171, Diana Laurillard, Fig. 6.1)

interaction among the participants on two levels: the discursive level which focuses on theory and conception, and the experiential level which addresses practice and activity. On the discursive level, the interaction occurs in a communicative way, while it is conducted in an adaptive way on the experiential level. For example, on the discursive level, a teacher provides the theory and concept of the task, and the learners inquire or express their own ideas, through which they might reach a full understanding of the task. In an experiential task, on the other hand, the learner attempts to reach the goal of the task based on the conceptual understanding of the task conducted on the discursive level. Figure 2.3 shows a Conversational Framework from Laurillard (2007), which Sharples et al. (2010) find suitable to adapt to mobile learning.

Mobile devices could serve as the media to connect learners with their partners, facilitating the process of coming to know through the conversation (Sharples 2005; Sharples et al. 2007). Laurillard in turn envisions that mobile learning technologies "offer exciting new opportunities for teachers to place learners in challenging active learning environments, making their own contributions, sharing ideas, exploring, investigating, experimenting, discussing" (2007, p. 174).

Pachler et al. (2010) also propose a perspective on mobile learning that is different from the traditional knowledge-transmitting style of learning. They define learning with mobile devices as a sociocultural ecology, with an interrelationship among three key components: (1) sociocultural structures, (2) cultural practices, and (3) the agency of mobile users, which they define as the mobile complex. Seipold and Pachler (2011) flesh out the three components as (1) digital media, technologies and systems, (2) things people do, and (3) human capacity to act in the world. In

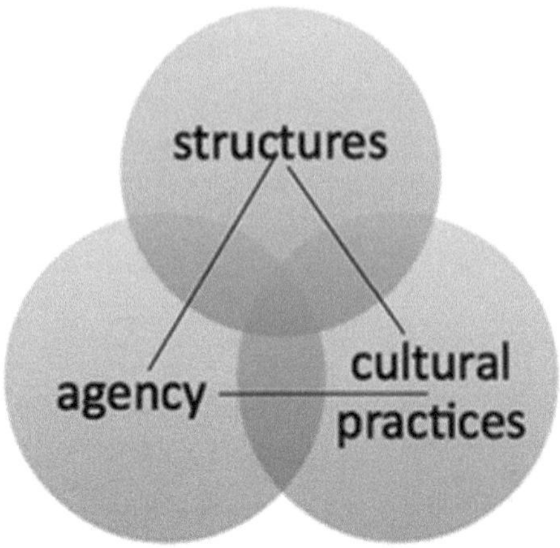

Fig. 2.4 Sociocultural ecology approach to mobile learning (Mobile Learning: Structures, Agency, Practice. Charting the Conceptual Space, 2010, p. 25, Fig. 1.4, Norbert Pachler, Ben Bachmair and John Cook. With permission of Springer)

this ecological framework, illustrated in Fig. 2.4, mobile devices help learners to understand ways to use their everyday life-worlds as learning spaces that everyone can access via their own mobile devices. Learning is conceived by Pachler et al. (2010) as a process of meaning-making or appropriation among these three components, claiming that the appropriation of the three components occurring in an educational context will trigger effective learning.

Figure 2.5 shows a model of L2 learning with mobile devices developed for the purposes of this book based on the approach discussed above. Teachers and learners interact with each other, through their mobile devices, at a place for discussion developed in cyberspace, all of which is regarded as a "community of practice" (Lave and Wenger 1991). Each learner or teacher contributes a context generated by their own life-world and communicates their perspectives with the others by socializing, networking, discussing, and negotiating. Through the interaction in the community of practice, they realize new insights. The affordances of m-learning lead to a form of learning defined by Sharples et al. (2007) as "the processes of coming to know through conversations across multiple contexts among people and personal interactive technologies" (p. 225). Seipold and Pachler (2011) state that the goal of mobile learning is to "be able to operate successfully in and across, new and ever changing contexts and learning spaces" (p. 3). Learners in the community of practice develop their knowledge with help from more skillful peers within the zone of proximal development as in the sociocultural theory pioneered by Vygotsky (1978).

Such interaction among learning community members can also be termed a collaborative dialogue (Swain 2000), a learner-centered dialogue where they are "engaged in problem solving and knowledge building" (p. 102). They can also realize, for instance through L2 communication, gaps in the linguistic knowledge of

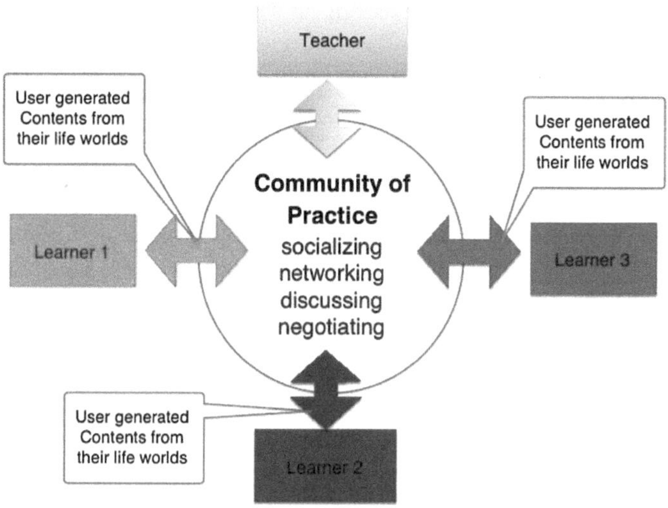

Fig. 2.5 Pedagogical model of mobile language learning

other members, leading to their focus more on their input and output to fill the gaps (Swain and Lapkin 2000). According to Watanabe and Swain (2007), Vygotsky's theory regards output just as a message to be sent to other members, but a collaborative dialogue perspective regards output as "a tool of cognitive activity that mediates L2 learning" (p. 121). That is to say, the meaningful interaction can make a member realize linguistic gaps, which tends to make his or her output more proficient through the effort to fill a gap. By keeping members connected where they would otherwise be separated in different locations, mobile devices can facilitate such collaborative dialogue. Members can act as autonomous agents in the online community of practice, bringing resources from their life-worlds into the community, and interacting with each other freely, at their own pace, which may be more difficult to realize in a classroom with its physical and temporal bounds, institutional culture, and psychosocial inhibitions. In the process of interacting, particularly in their L2, in order to connect with peers, members would need to analyze the input, access their linguistic knowledge, and, as a result, try to make their output linguistically more sophisticated and competent. The next chapter will present two types of case studies where mobile technology was utilized to set up such L2 learning communities. Mobile learning is just beginning to cross over from personal uses by students to being harnessed by educational institutions.

As discussed above, mobile learning pedagogy should pay more attention to its network function to connect learners with each other online. In L2 education it seems inevitable to focus not only on interaction but also on language itself, so as to validate the effectiveness of a certain way of learning. This is because the L2 improvement tends to be measured by language competence such as the amount of vocabulary, with the seemingly inarguable verdict rendered by standardized tests. In the next chapter, nevertheless, experiments harnessing the ubiquitous mobile phones carried by students will be shown, focusing on the interaction with peers. The results will test the hypothesis developed in this chapter that L2 interaction focusing mainly on meaning-making can enhance English language competence even as expressed by scores on TOEIC® tests and the quality of essay writing. Does there always need to be a focus on the form of language or teaching explicit items when L2 is the very medium through which learners overcome their physical separation and connect with peers, which inter alia is both a motive and a goal?

References

Al-Seghayer, K. (2001). The effect of multimedia annotation modes on L2 vocabulary acquisition: a comparative study. *Language Learning and Technology, 5*(1), 202–232.

Brown, G. (1990). Cultural values: The interpretation of discourse. *ELT Journal, 38*(4), 233–241.

Chapelle, C. A. (1998). Multimedia CALL: Lessons to be learned from research on instructed SLA. *Language Learning & Technology, 2*(1), 22–34.

Chun, D. L., & Plass, J. L. (1996). Effects of multimedia annotations on vocabulary acquisition. *Modern Language Journal, 80*(2), 183–198.

Derakhshan, A., & Khodabakhshzadeh, H. (2011). Why CALL why not MALL: An in-depth review of text-message vocabulary learning. *Theory and Practice in Language Studies, 1*(9), 1150–1159.

FastAsk. (2014, October 10). Monthly fixed-point investigation about mobile devices and social media in September 2014. Retrieved from https://www.fast-ask.com/report/report-monthly-20141010.html

Khamkhien, A. (2012). Demystifying Thai EFL learners' perceptual learning style preferences. *The Southeast Asian Journal of English Language Studies, 18*(1), 61–74.

Kindai University. (2013, February 8). *Daigakusei no jouhoukikiriou ni kansuru chousa* [An investigation of college students' ownership of information technology devices]. Retrieved from http://www.kindai.ac.jp/130208.pdf

Kozulin, A. (2003). Psychological tools and mediated learning. In A. Kozulin, B. Gindis, & V. S. Ageyev (Eds.), *Vygotsky's educational theory in cultural context* (pp. 15–38). Cambridge: Cambridge University Press.

Krashen, S. (1982). *Principles and practice in second language acquisition.* Oxford: Pergamon.

Krashen, S. (1985). *The input hypothesis.* London: Longman.

Kubota, R. (2002). Language teaching in Japan. In D. Block & D. Cameron (Eds.), *Globalization and language teaching* (pp. 13–28). London: Routledge.

Kukulska-Hulme, A. (2009). Will mobile learning change language learning? *ReCALL, 21*(2), 157–165.

Laufer, B., & Hill, M. (2000). What lexical information do L2 learners select in a CALL dictionary and how does it affect word retention? *Language Learning & Technology, 3*, 58–76.

Laufer, B., & Hulstijn, J. (2001). Incidental vocabulary acquisition in a second language: The construct of task-induced involvement. *Applied Linguistics, 22*(1), 1–26.

Laurillard, D. (2002). *Rethinking university teaching: A framework for the effective use of educational technology*. London: Routledge.

Laurillard, D. (2007). Pedagogical forms for mobile learning: Framing research questions. In N. Pachler (Ed.), *Mobile learning: Towards a research agenda* (pp. 153–175). London: WLE Centre, the Institute of Education, University of London.

Lave, J., & Wenger, E. (1991). *Situated learning: Legitimate peripheral participation.* Cambridge, UK: Cambridge University Press.

Lee, M. J. W., & McLoughlin, C. (2007). Teaching and learning in the Web 2.0 era: Empowering students through learner-generated content. *International Journal of Instructional Technology and Distance Learning, 4*(10), 21–34.

Lomicka, L. (1998). To gloss or not to gloss: An investigation of reading comprehension online. *Language Learning & Technology, 1*(2), 41–50.

Lu, M. (2008). Effectiveness of vocabulary learning via mobile phone. *Journal of Computer Assisted learning, 24*, 515–525.

Ministry of Internal Affairs and Communications of Japan. (2015). *Heisei 26-nen joho tsushin media no riyo jikan to joho kodo ni kan suru chosa* [Research on time spent on IT media and behavior in fiscal year 2014]. Retrieved from http://www.soumu.go.jp/main_content/000357568.pdf

Pachler, N. (2001). Electronic reference tools for foreign language learners, teachers and users: Offline vocabulary look-up programs. *Language Learning Journal, 24*, 24–29.

Pachler, N., Bachmair, B., & Cook, J. (2010). *Mobile learning: Structures, agency, practices*. New York: Springer.

Sato, T., & Suzuki, A. (2010). Do multimedia-oriented visual glosses really facilitate EFL vocabulary learning?: A comparison of planar images with three-dimensional images. *Asian EFL Journal, 12*(4), 160–172.

Sato, T., & Suzuki, A. (2012). From a gloss to a learning tool: Do visual aids enhance better sentence comprehension? In L. Bradley & S. Thouësny (Eds.), *EuroCALL 2012 Proceedings* (pp. 264–268).

Sato, T., Matsunuma, M., & Suzuki, A. (2013). Enhancement of automatization through vocabulary learning using CALL: Can prompt language processing lead to better comprehension in L2 reading? *ReCALL, 25*(1), 143–158.

Seipold, J., & Pachler, N. (2011). Evaluating mobile learning practice. *MedienPädagogik–Zeitschrift für Theorie und Praxis der Medienbildung, 19*.

Sfard, A. (1998). On two metaphors for learning and the danger of choosing just one. *Educational Researcher, 27*(2), 4–13.

Sharples, M. (2005). Learning as conversation: Transforming education in the mobile age. *Proceedings of the conference on seeing, understanding, learning in the mobile age* (pp. 147–152).

Sharples, M., Taylor, J., & Vavoula, G. (2005). Towards a theory of mobile learning. *Proceedings of mLearn 2005, 1*(1), 1–9.

Sharples, M., Taylor, J., & Vavoula, G. (2007). A theory of learning for the mobile age. In R. Andrews & C. Haythornthwaite (Eds.), *The Sage handbook of elearning research* (pp. 221–247). London: Sage.

Sharples, M., Taylor, J., & Vavoula, G. (2010). A theory of learning for the mobile age. In *Medienbildung in neuen Kulturräumen* (pp. 87–99). VS Verlag für Sozialwissenschaften.

Shirai, Y. (2011). Gaikokugo gakushuu no kagaku (Scientific verification of foreign language learning and teaching). *Memoirs of Kyushu International University, 6*(1–2), 145–174.

Schutz, A., & Luckmann, T. (1973). *The structures of the life-world* (Vol. 1). Evanston, IL: Northwestern University Press.

So, H. J. (2012). Turning on mobile learning in Asia: Illustrative initiatives and policy implications. *Policy Focus: UNESCO Working Paper Series on Mobile Learning, 1*, 1–32.

Stockwell, G., & Hubbard, P. (2013). *Some emerging principles for mobile-assisted language learning*. Monterey, CA: The International Research Foundation for English Language Education. Retrieved from http://www.tirfonline.org/english-in-the-workforce/mobile-assisted-language-learning

Swain, M. (2000). The output hypothesis and beyond: Mediating acquisition through collaborative dialogue. In J. Lantolf (Ed.), *Sociocultural approaches to second language research* (pp. 97–115). Oxford: Oxford University Press.

Swain, M., & Lapkin, S. (2000). Task-based second language learning: The uses of the first language. *Language Teaching Research, 4*, 251–274.

Tanaka, T. (2009). Communicative language teaching and its cultural appropriateness in Japan. *Doshisha Studies in English*, 84, 107–123. Retrieved from http://doors.doshisha.ac.jp/webopac/bdyview.do?bodyid=BD00013255&elmid=Body&lfname=020000840005.pdf

Vygotsky, L. S. (1978). Mind in society: The development of higher psychological processes (M. Cole, V. John-Steiner, S. Scribner & E. Souberman., Eds.). (A. R. Luria, M. Lopez-Morillas & M. Cole [with J. V. Wertsch], Trans.). Cambridge, MA: Harvard University Press. (Original manuscripts [ca. 1930–1934]).

Watanabe, Y., & Swain, M. (2007). Effects of proficiency difference and patterns of pair interaction on second language learning: Collaborative dialogue between adult ESL learners. *Language Teaching Research, 11*(2), 121–142.

Wenger, E. (2011). Communities of practice: A brief introduction. Retrieved from https://scholarsbank.uoregon.edu/xmlui/bitstream/handle/1794/11736/A%20brief%20introduction%20to%20CoP.pdf?sequence=1

Yoshii, M., & Fraitz, J. (2002). Second language incidental vocabulary retention: The effect of text and picture annotation types. *CALICO Journal, 20*(1), 33–58.

Yeh, Y., & Wang, C. (2003). Effects of multimedia vocabulary annotations and learning styles on vocabulary learning. *CALICO Journal, 21*(1), 131–144.

Chapter 3
Tokyo University of Agriculture and Technology Case Study: Smartphone App LINE for EFL Peer Learning

Abstract The first of three case studies in this book addresses online interaction in EFL with smartphones via LINE, a communication tool that is free and familiar to Japanese students. This chapter introduces two kinds of group interactions aimed to accord with both sociocultural theory and the psychological contours of students in the instructor's culture. First, learners wrote L2 messages and posted them on a closed group board in LINE. In the second experiment, a bot instantly and automatically translated L1 messages they posted into L2. After their one-month interactions, both groups showed improvement of their English language competence in both receptive and productive skills. The results of the questionnaire also proclaimed their active participation with positive feedback about the L2 online interaction.

Institutional Context

Founded in 1949, Tokyo University of Agriculture and Technology (TUAT) is a relatively small-scale national university located in the suburbs of Tokyo. TUAT has about 4200 undergraduates and a relatively large proportion of graduate students, about 1800, including about 400 foreign students. It has only two faculties: agriculture and technology. Although only around 800 freshmen enroll in TUAT each year, there are in total 13 departments: eight in technology and five in agriculture. The faculty of technology includes, for instance, life sciences, mechanical systems engineering, and computer and information science, whereas the faculty of agriculture includes environmental and natural resource science, biological production, and veterinary medicine. TUAT serves not only undergraduates but also offers postgraduate programs toward master's and doctoral degrees.

Since the institution is regarded as a research-oriented university, many of the undergraduates go on to TUAT postgraduate schools to continue their research. Their main concern, therefore, is to conduct their research, because many of them have the desire to be scientists or engineers rather than office workers. The institution is trying to catch the wave of globalization and therefore wants the students

S. McCarty et al., *Implementing Mobile Language Learning Technologies in Japan*, SpringerBriefs in Education, DOI 10.1007/978-981-10-2451-1_3

to be "global human resources" who can fluently communicate with non-Japanese in English as well as handle scientific work. This is despite the fact that there is no urgent need for them to use English in their daily lives. They must maintain a busy schedule doing many tasks such as experiments in their laboratories, practical training on farms or in animal hospitals, writing many reports, attending various lectures related to their major subject, and so forth, where the Japanese language suffices. As a result, learning English tends to be thought of as a secondary task.

As the university only has departments related to agriculture and technology, the students are not specializing in English or liberal arts. The setting for English learning is that students take some English courses during their first two years as one of the compulsory subjects to earn a bachelor's degree in their own major.

However, some students keep learning English autonomously for their research activities or job hunting. There is considerable motivation among the student body to learn English, as they have rather clear goals to learn English for their future career as scientists or engineers. More than half of TUAT undergraduates go on to graduate schools in order to continue their research and to earn higher degrees. They therefore recognize the fact that they are going to encounter opportunities to use English, because at the very least they are forced to read journals, write reports and papers, and make presentations about their research in English. In that sense, they might understand the importance of achieving a higher level of English language competence to carry out research activities even when they are undergraduates. As a matter of fact, however, only a small number of English lectures provide a chance to study English, and their autonomous exposure to English might not be frequent, because learning English becomes secondary compared to their research in their laboratories, on farms or in animal hospitals.

Technological Context

Campus IT Infrastructure

TUAT has a relatively robust IT infrastructure. A Wireless Network System is available in and around the lecture rooms. Also there are three rooms with desktop PCs. This means that the students can freely access the Internet anywhere on campus and also utilize various kinds of software such as Microsoft Office, the Moodle learning management system, and so on, once they log in with their ID number and password. However, this infrastructure might not affect their language learning environment very much. PC labs are not used for language classes, because the number of the PC rooms is few, and the capacity of each PC room is around 80, which is too big to conduct classes for language learning. Furthermore, many language teachers prohibit students from connecting to the Internet with their mobile devices during classes, even though most of the classrooms have a Wi-Fi router to connect to the campus network system, because the devices might be used as a tool for cheating, such as by using translation software (e.g., Google translation) in a writing task. For such reasons, IT services and facilities installed at TUAT are not likely to be used for language classes.

Hardware/Devices Available

Considering the above constraints on utilizing the campus IT infrastructure for language learning, Sato decided not to utilize the devices installed at TUAT but rather those that students already owned, namely mobile devices such as feature phones, smartphones, and tablets. As discussed in Chap. 2, almost all the university students in Japan have their own mobile devices, so they have been using them in their everyday life: browsing Websites, receiving and sending messages, uploading photos or movies on their SNS sites, and so on. This means that no special facility and expertise is needed to use their mobile devices even for academic purposes. As Kukulska-Hulme (2009) points out, one of the advantages of learning with mobile devices is ownership, which means that every mobile owner could fairly access the resources anytime and anywhere they want. In the case of countries like Japan, it means that university students are similarly equipped to access educational resources anytime and anywhere.

However, before implementing mobile-based learning, teachers should consider whether all their students own some kind of mobile device (Kukulska-Hulme et al. 2015). This is because there are students who are unable or unwilling to carry a mobile device, due to the expense, for example, or to avoid the temptation to be distracted from important work. Therefore, only software applications that are available not only for mobile devices but also for personal computers should be implemented formally by educators. Students without mobile devices should be able to access sufficient resources and submit their work from personal computers at home or in PC rooms if they are assigned tasks with a certain application. To maintain fair accessibility of resources via computing devices, educators should not assume that every student has a mobile device, but rather develop alternative ways for students to accomplish the same learning goals.

Implementation

Theoretical Framework

As discussed in the previous chapter, there are two perspectives on learning: one is that learning refers to the process of knowledge acquisition, whereas the other is that learning is the process of coming to know (Sharples et al. 2007) or meaning-making (Pachler et al. 2010) in the course of interactions within a community of practice, based on the premise that both teachers and learners play an active part in conducting language learning (Kukulska-Hulme et al. 2015). The latter theory supports a practice of peer social m-learning whereby mobile devices enhance not only knowledge acquisition but also interaction within a community of practice. Similar ownership of mobile devices brings about a fair accessibility of resources, and allows students to bring resources from their own life-world into the community of practice, which helps students to contextualize their learning in their own settings. Pachler et al. (2010) state that adding context to what is learned allows for deeper understanding and richer meaning-making. Thus, the process of interaction in English, which enables participants to communicate in terms of the resources from their own life-worlds, is hypothesized to facilitate learners' L2 competence as well as the processes of coming to know and making meaning.

EFL Learning Goals

The goal of this study with mobile devices was to enhance students' English language competence, especially their literacy, in the process of interacting with other students online. Through their interactions in the target language of English, it was hypothesized that their English language competence, especially reading and writing, would be enhanced, even though the practice is not like knowledge acquisition, which is the mainstream practice of English language teaching and learning in Japan. The advantage of L2 interaction practices this study implements is theoretically backed by Swain's collaborative dialogues (2000) and Long's Interaction Hypothesis (1996), both of which underline the importance of interactions to develop L2 proficiency. Meanwhile, conducting such practices with mobile devices, as discussed in Chap. 2, could bring out the learner autonomy Asian students are capable of because of the characteristic of mobile learning. Therefore, this study could hypothesize that peer mobile learning leads to learners' active and continued participation in the L2 interaction.

m-Learning Initiatives/Innovations

The learning technologies utilized in this case study are merely the mobile devices each participant owns and the LINE application that they had already installed. Considering that LINE has been one of the most downloaded mobile applications among Japanese (LINE Corporate Announcement 2016), the college students, all of whom own their own mobile devices (Kindai University 2013), should be accustomed to the application enough to receive messages from others and post their messages with photos or stamps. The ubiquity of LINE is indispensable for using it formally in an institutional setting for m-learning. The LINE group chat function was selected as the main forum for student interactions.

As an application that can be utilized both in PCs and mobile devices, LINE was chosen for class interactions reported in this chapter. LINE is one of the most popular applications for online communication not only in Japan but also in the world. The top four countries which have active users are Japan, Taiwan, Thailand, and Indonesia (LINE Corporate Announcement 2016). According to a press release from LINE on April 2, 2014, more than 400 million people had registered as a user of this application (LINE News 2014). On October 10, 2014, LINE announced that more than 560 million people had registered, while there existed 170 million active users (Mainichi Daily News 2014) and 215 million by the end of 2015 (LINE Corporate Announcement 2016), despite the fact that the service had launched on June 23, 2011.

There might be several reasons why LINE has dramatically become popular. The first reason is that LINE is basically a free application. After downloading it from the Website, people can communicate with others, not only one-to-one but also among group members. Also they can communicate combining text with photos, emoticons, stamps or animations. Communicating by plural modes such as words and symbols of feelings has a kind of similarity to face-to-face communication, which is one of the prominent features that differentiate LINE from other communication tools.

In fact, LINE has become the most frequently used online communication tool in Japan. According to a report of ICT use in Japan (Ministry of Internal Affairs and Communication of Japan 2015), 77.9 % of the teenagers have already used LINE and 90.5 % of those in their twenties used LINE in the fiscal year 2014, while 25.9 % of the teenagers and 61.1 % of those in their twenties used Facebook, and 49.3 and 53.8 %, respectively, used Twitter.

Furthermore, the variety of devices and operating systems (OS) on which LINE is available is another advantage of this application. The chat data on LINE can be synchronized with PCs such as Windows, Mac and Linux, which enables LINE users to continue interacting with others even though the device is changed in the course of the interaction. In that sense, they can use LINE flexibly in whatever way they wish. Such advantages have attracted most of the mobile phone users in Japan to utilize LINE in their daily life.

There is another advantage of using LINE for academic purposes, compared with other social media such as Facebook or Twitter. Users can conduct a closed group chat without the interference of extraneous messages and other contacts. LINE has a function to make a group where only those invited by the group representative can join the interaction, and others cannot access the group. Stockwell and Hubbard (2013) introduced a case where learners hesitated to use their private SNS accounts for academic use; they preferred to draw a clear line between academic and private use of their SNS. With LINE, on the other hand, it would be easier to distinguish between private and academic use with one account due to the fact that other users could not see all of one's friends or groups. The interaction of a group is private, so no other people can access the content, and therefore the participants of the group can feel comfortable interacting with each other.

It is also true, on the other hand, that m-learning in general, and particularly in a language like Japanese, faces considerable challenges. One of the obstacles is the difficulty of reading and writing, especially lengthy texts, on the small screens of mobile devices (Stockwell and Hubbard 2013). Furthermore, the difference in the ways to input English and Japanese makes m-learning more challenging in Japan. English is usually typed with a QWERTY keyboard not only in PCs but also in mobile phones. Yet in Japan there are not many mobile users who type with a QWERTY keyboard; instead, people tend to use a flick keyboard designed for the Japanese language whose alignment is completely different from that of the QWERTY keyboard. In fact, even the QWERTY keyboard is less suited to typing letters on mobile phones because of small buttons to push in typing letters, leading to many typing mistakes, so anyone might hesitate to write much English with their mobile phones.

However, LINE has a solution for this challenge, as the use of LINE is available not only for mobile phones but also for PCs. The log of an interaction with others is synchronized, so they can conduct the interaction via LINE with whatever device and whichever keyboard they utilize. This is a merit of using LINE in mobile learning. Note, however, that all the conversation logs are saved in the mobile version, whereas the log data are deleted after just two weeks in the PC version.

Administrative Challenges/Student Training

One of the advantages of the implementation of mobile learning in institutional settings is that the institutions do not have to install any computer facilities such as personal computers and Internet connections. That is because most students already have their own mobile devices such as feature phones or smart phones, and they are able to access any resources on the Internet without help from the institution. In the case of this experiment, LINE was already regarded as an essential application for mobile users among the cohort of university students.

As this practice was conducted independently of lectures, without utilizing any kind of IT infrastructure at TUAT, no administrative or other support was needed from the institution. As it was carried out with a small cohort, the language teacher could handle all the administrative, pedagogical, and technological issues involved in the practice.

Procedure 1

Seven university students participated in this experiment. They responded to an advertisement on campus for students willing to learn English utilizing their own mobile devices for no credit. Participants were two postgraduates and five undergraduates from the faculty of engineering, from different departments such as life sciences, chemical sciences, mechanical engineering, and information technology. This shows that they were not specializing in English studies, but their English language competence ranged between lower and upper intermediate level, enough to understand English sentences other members posted and to write their own English sentences in LINE.

Prior to the experiment, all of the participants were assembled in the investigator's office for orientation. First of all, Sato appointed a postgraduate student as a facilitator, who gave the other members a chance to introduce themselves. After the face-to-face self-introductions as an icebreaker, Sato explained what they were going to do: interact in English via their mobile devices for a month; taking turns posting topics and sharing their ideas and opinions on LINE.

TOEIC© tests and essay writing tasks were conducted before and after the one-month interaction, except that those who had taken the same test within a few months did not have to take the pre-test. The essay writing tasks were short essays within 30 min, without referring to any resources such as dictionaries. In addition, students were asked to answer a questionnaire about the interactions after the period was over.

The participants were asked to keep interacting with other members in English via the group chats, where communication is possible only with the people registered as group members on LINE. Each of them were to join the community of practice by posting text messages, photos, stamps, and so on. The topic for the interaction was supposed to be decided by one of the members every few days. The topic could be related to their daily life to make the interaction smooth even while using English as a foreign language. Based on the topic posted by a member in the online community, interactions with other members should be necessary, such as sharing ideas and photos or movies, discussing and negotiating, all of which are similar to daily social activities (see Fig. 3.1). If members introduced their hometown, for example, others would be expected to share information about their own hometown, through texts, photos, and the like, introducing new information, asking questions to each other, and answering. After finishing the interaction about a certain topic, another person was supposed to post a different topic. This cycle was to be continued during the month-long period. Participants were asked to write at least three posts every weekday, but they were also allowed to post on weekends. When the cycle seemed stuck, the facilitator was to take the initiative in posting messages and encourage the others to post. This cycle was repeated.

Assessment of Effectiveness

Experimental Results

Here are the results of the month of interactions. As shown in Fig. 3.2, for the 24 days which at least one post could be found, the total number of the posts that were submitted on LINE was 533. This averages out to 23 total posts per day, 76 posts per person during the month, and 3.3 posts per person per day. The maximum number of posts in a day was 55 (Day 2), whereas the minimum number was 2

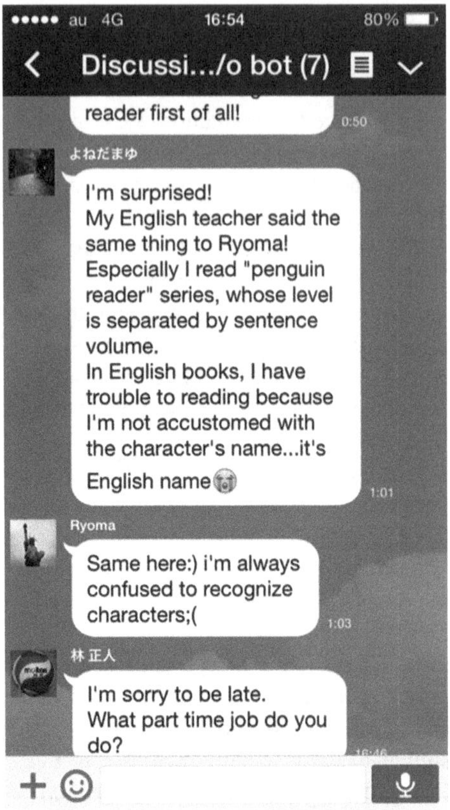

Fig. 3.1 Example of an interaction via LINE

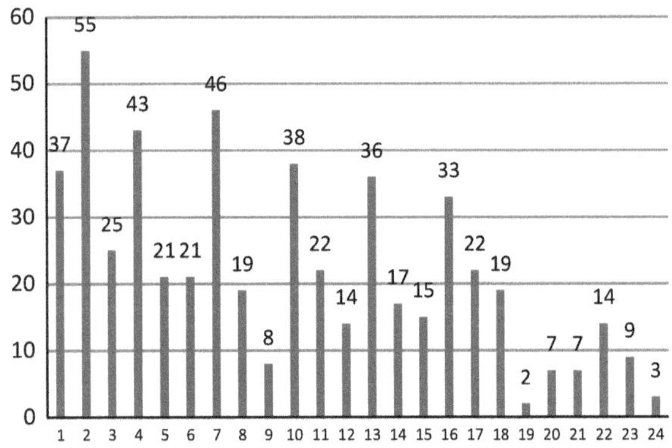

Fig. 3.2 Number of posts to LINE

(Day 19). In the final few days, few posts were submitted, as students had to take final term examinations during that period.

In terms of the number of the English words they posted, a similar trend can be seen (see Fig. 3.3). The total number of words they posted during the period was

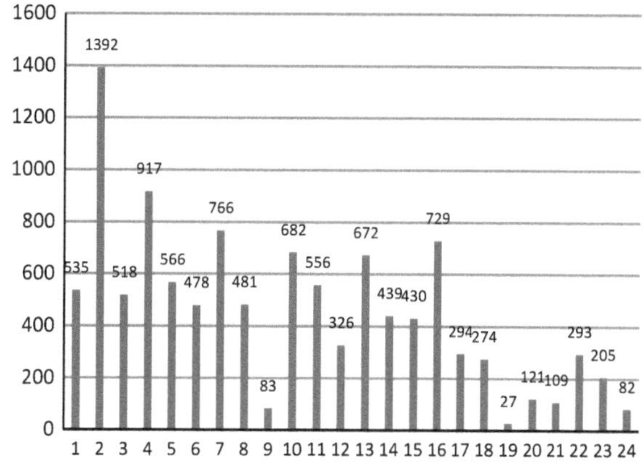

Fig. 3.3 Total words posted

10,975. This means that an average of 457 words were posted per day, 1568 words per person and 65 words per person per day. The maximum number of total words was 1392 on Day 2, whereas the minimum number was 27 on Day 19. For the first few days, they wrote many English words, but the total number declined, especially during the final week.

The number of posts according to the participants is shown in Fig. 3.4. The largest number of posts submitted by one participant was 108 (Member 1), while the smallest was 49 (Member 6). As for the total words they posted, shown in the following Fig. 3.5, the results were similar: Member 1, who posted most frequently reached 3539 words, while Member 7, who posted the least frequently, wrote 896 words, which was one-fourth of Member 1's output.

Results of TOEIC© tests before and after the interactions are shown in Fig. 3.6. Among seven participants, five members improved their scores, but two members decreased. The average score of their pre-test was 525.2, whereas that of their post-test was 528.6, amounting to an average improvement of 3.6. As for the reading section in the following Fig. 3.7, 4 members improved their scores, 2 declined, and 2 were unchanged. The average score of their pre-test was 248.6,

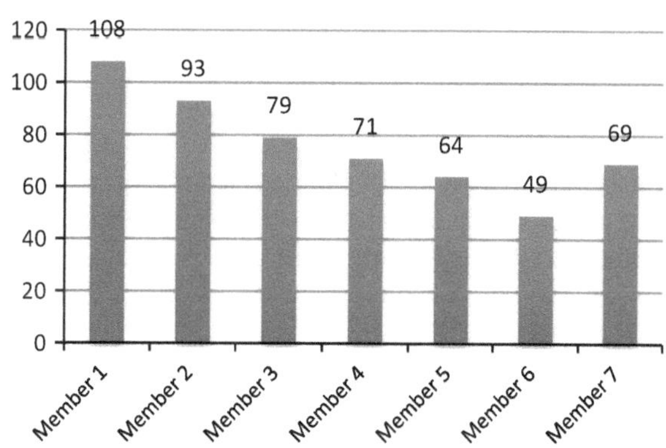

Fig. 3.4 Number of posts by individual members

Fig. 3.5 Total words posted by individual members

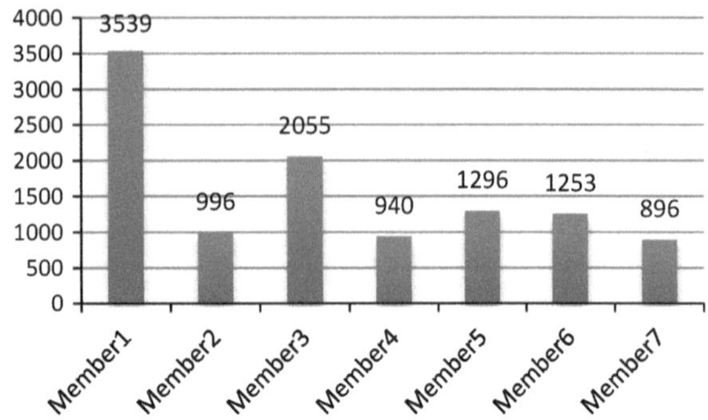

Fig. 3.6 Individual TOEIC test whole scores

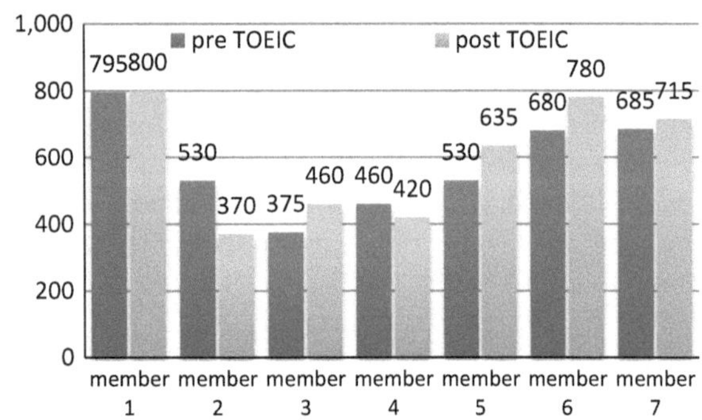

Fig. 3.7 TOEIC scores (reading section only)

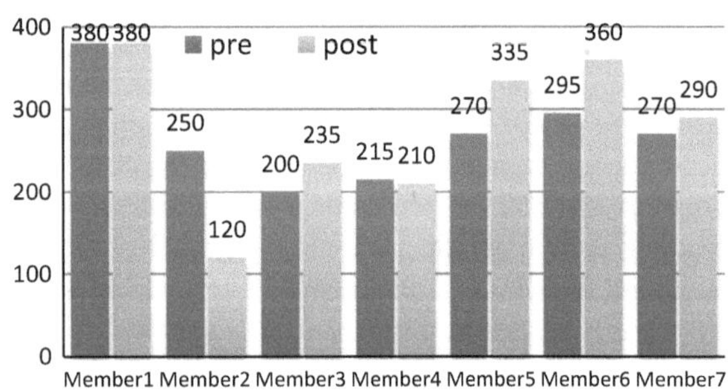

whereas that of their post-test was 240. The improvement in their reading scores after the online interaction provides one indication that the interaction had a somewhat positive effect on the overall English language literacy of the group.

Further, at the individual level, the number of the words they posted and their reading section scores are compared. As seen in Fig. 3.8, some correlations can be discerned. Those who posted many words on LINE tended to improve their TOEIC© scores. The reading score of Member 3, for example, who posted 2055 words (the second most words of the seven members), improved from 200 to 235. Conversely, those whose scores decreased were ones who had posted relatively

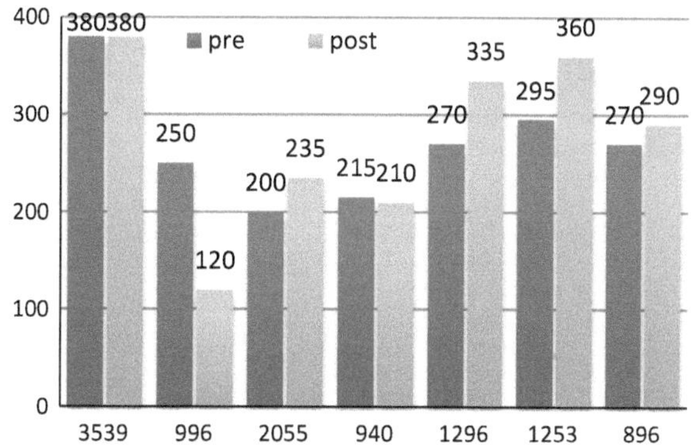

Fig. 3.8 Comparison between reading scores and total words posted

fewer words. Member 2, for example, who posted the second least amount (996 words), declined from 250 to 120. The coefficient of correlation between the number of posts and the scores of the post TOEIC reading section was 0.50, which might indicate a positive correlation to some degree. The positive correlation, whereby members who posted more words tended to scored better in reading than those who posted fewer words, could perhaps be explained by the extent to which they built up their vocabulary, reading comprehension, and overall literacy in the process of reading and writing sentences during the interactions.

Next, the essays the participants wrote before and after the interaction are analyzed in terms of their readability and average length of a sentence, hypothesizing that this interaction would give them more opportunities to read and write English sentences and, as a result, make their sentences longer and more complex. First of all, the readability of each essay was calculated according to ARI (the Automated Readability Index) scores, one of the main measurements for readability. As seen in Fig. 3.9, six essays showed increased readability scores (Members 1, 2, 3, 4, 5 and 7), while one essay remained constant (Members 6).

However, as for the average length of a sentence in their essays, six out of seven (Members 1, 2, 3, 5, 6, and 7) increased the number of the words per sentence. Moreover, in comparing the average words in a sentence and the difference of the TOEIC© scores before and after the interaction, those whose TOEIC scores

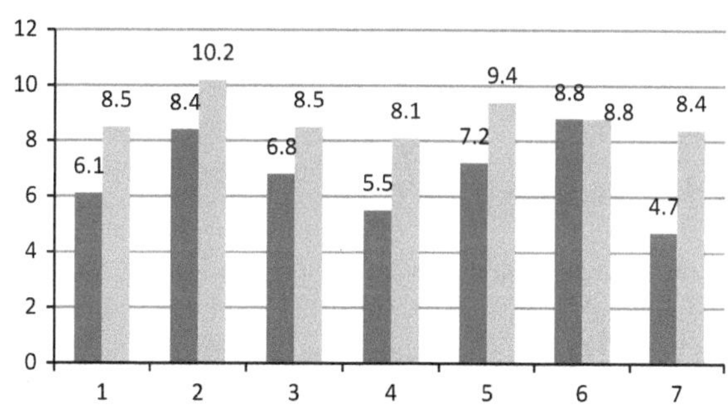

Fig. 3.9 Readability of the essays

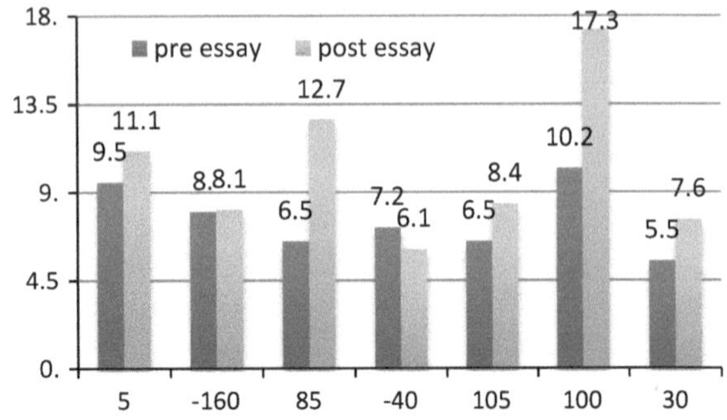

Fig. 3.10 Change in average sentence length compared to the difference between total pre- and post- TOEIC© test scores (plus or minus at the bottom of columns)

increased could write longer sentences. Figure 3.10 also shows that those who did not improve the TOEIC© scores (member 2 and 4), did not write longer sentences than they did before the interaction.

Discussion of the Experimental Results

The figures above illustrate that those who posted more writing during the period of the experiment tended not only to get higher TOEIC© scores, but also to write more sophisticated and longer sentences in their essays after the interactions. Although no measure of statistical validity was conducted due to the small number of participants, these findings might indicate that active participation in interactions in the community of practice positively affected their TOEIC scores or literacy skills involved in writing better and longer sentences. That is, their L2 competence may have been enhanced through the interaction of the community of practice formed in cyberspace, despite the fact that no particular target language was assigned to them and there was no explicit focus on vocabulary or grammar. That could be a reason for the positive correlation found between the amount of L2 interactive activity through mobile devices and enhanced L2 competence as shown in some cases by improvements in TOEIC reading scores and in written essays.

It seems logical that the ongoing output in the target language would lead to the production of longer sentences, but the findings raise the further question why the quality of the sentences including vocabulary and grammar also was improved without explicit instruction. The answer this question might be inferred from the feedback of the participants, shown in the following section.

Follow-up Questionnaire Results

No statistical analysis was carried out for the mobile-based language learning, due to the small cohort. Therefore, no unequivocal conclusion can be derived from the findings. However, another type of data was gathered to analyze the effectiveness of this practice with mobile devices. Questionnaire research was conducted after all the tasks to reflect on the practices students engaged in for 1 month. The data may be suggestive of ways to implement similar mobile-based L2 interaction tasks in other local settings.

The questionnaire first asked about the frequency of checking posts to the LINE group from other members. Two students answered "very often," four answered "often," and one answered "sometimes."

Then, they were asked to describe the willingness with which they submitted posts. One student answered "willingly," five answered "rather willingly," and one answered "rather unwillingly."

They were also asked to describe how they felt when answering questions asked by other members directly during the online interactions. Three answered "willingly," 3 answered "rather willingly," and 1 answered "rather unwillingly."

Asked what they thought about the online interaction in English, the result was that all participants enjoyed the task: Five answered "enjoyable," while two answered "rather enjoyable." They were also asked to write their reason, as follows [their comments are translated into English by Sato]:

- No fixed topic allowed us to talk freely and comfortably.
- Being exposed to various English expressions from others could make my English skills improve.
- It was a good practice to compare the English expressions I wrote with those the others wrote.
- I enjoyed interacting with the other members by discussing various topics that would be useful in our life.
- It was enjoyable because we could chat with the others in English, as we do with our first language.
- I have never participated in such an interaction. I felt it was innovative.

The final question was if they agreed that this online discussion would be useful in learning English. They all answered positively: Five agreed and two somewhat agreed. The reasons they thought so were as follows [Sato translation]:

- It became a trigger to learn English for communication.
- I found I could make myself understood in English to some extent.
- I was sometimes irritated because I could not express what I intended during the interaction, but such experience motivated me to study English more.
- By looking up words in dictionaries before posting my comments to participate in the interaction, I could improve my vocabulary and grammar.
- I enjoyed the process to express what I wanted to say.
- Reading the posts from the other members was very useful.

Discussion of the Questionnaire Results

To sum up, despite the fact that Japanese L2 learners tend to be passive and not try to express their own ideas in classroom-based activities, this kind of interaction where each member interacts through their mobile devices might change their attitude to be more active. The questionnaire results showed that they rather actively checked the others' posts and willingly tried to respond to them. They also seemed to enjoy participating in this activity, so more positive attitudes are liable to lead to more successful L2 learning even after such an experiment.

Students were not explicitly taught English as usual, such as vocabulary and grammar, during the practice, but the comments showed that they tried to make their sentences grammatical and comprehensible in order to make themselves understood in English, by referring to dictionaries or by reading others' posts. A comment to an open-ended question showed that, despite the fact that no linguistic knowledge or feedback was given by the teacher during the practice, they tried to make their sentences grammatical and comprehensible in order to make themselves understood in English by autonomously referring to dictionaries ("By looking up dictionaries before posting my comments to participate in the interaction, I could improve my vocabulary and grammar") or by reading others' posts ("Reading the posts from the other members was very useful"). This may suggest that the interactions focused the learners on coming to know, making meaning, or what Swain (2000) termed collaborative dialogue, which in turn led to enhancing the learners' awareness of language structure, because the interaction motivated them to correctly express their intended meaning.

Compared with face-to-face interaction, which requires a spontaneous response, mobile-based interaction gives interlocutors some time to refer to dictionaries or reference books before answering others' inquiries. As a result of this process of making meaning, their target language competence might be improved. What is more, the process was felt to be enjoyable, for example "to express what I wanted to say," or to "make myself understood in English to some extent." On the other hand, it was also motivating even to be spurred by "irritation" at the difficulty thereof "to study English more." In this view, their eagerness to express themselves in English could enhance their L2 competence, not because of language knowledge provided by teachers or materials, but rather by the imperatives of interacting with others, indirectly enhancing their literacy.

Challenges and a Possible Solution

According to the findings from the L2 interaction with LINE, it is found that more interactions with others via mobile devices might enhance English language competence despite the fact that no linguistic knowledge was given by the teacher. But still there are challenges to implement mobile-based interaction tasks.

As mentioned above, typing English might sometimes be troublesome for young Japanese L2 learners (Stockwell and Hubbard 2013). It might be true that they have gotten used to typing letters with mobile devices through using email and SMS, or communicating on some SNS sites. However, the way to type Japanese characters is different from that of English. English sentences tend to be typed on a QWERTY keyboard, which is available on PCs and some mobile devices. Japanese young people, however, have used mobile devices more often than PCs, as the data in Chap. 2 illustrate, so they prefer to use flick input rather than the QWERTY keyboard. According to unrecorded conversations with some college students, they indicated that writing English sentences made them irritated due to using the QWERTY keyboard on such a small screen, and this made them type the sentences incorrectly, leading to their hesitation to join L2 interactions with their mobile devices.

Furthermore, writing as a productive skill could be regarded as one of the difficult skills for L2 learners to master, because it requires language processing with more mental effort than receptive skills such as reading (Swain 2000). As evidence of this, the comments from those involved in the interaction with LINE mentioned above showed that participants were worried whether they could write sentences without errors. This indicates that pressure to compose correct sentences tends to inhibit L2 learners from interacting with others, that is, without a supportive community of practice.

To tackle such technological and linguistic issues for mobile-based language learning, a solution should be developed to facilitate uninhibited interaction with others. One possible approach to this challenge is the Translation Bot, a function of LINE anyone can use for free.

The translation bot is a tool for communication available only in LINE. In communicating with others who use different languages, the bot mediates the text conversation by translating their chat into the target language. For example, Fig. 3.11 shows that the Japanese-English translation bot can translate messages written in Japanese into English right after each member posts it in a community. The translation bot in LINE is available not only between Japanese and English, but various kinds of translation bots are also available: Japanese–Korean, Japanese–Chinese, English–Spanish, English–French, English–Indonesian and so on. It is obvious, however, that these bots cannot always translate texts correctly, although the accuracy level improves as the bot keeps processing the language data, which makes subsequent translations more accurate. The English sentences the bot produced during this experiment seemed to be intelligible enough to get interlocutors' message across such that uninhibited interactions with others could be maintained.

Given the challenges of writing activities with a mobile device, this translation bot could facilitate smoother L2 interaction, compared with the previous practice where the participants had to type English sentences on a QWERTY keyboard. The following section will explain the details of the practice in detail.

Procedure 2

Although the procedures were mostly the same as the previous practice, engaging in interactions with other members via the LINE app installed in their own mobile devices, the participants were different. Seven university students participated in this practice. They were under- and postgraduate students from the faculty of engineering, who were not specializing in English-related subjects.

Fig. 3.11 Communication with the Japanese-English translation bot

As in the previous practice, the participants were asked to interact with others via LINE for one month (although their remarks were found on 21 days). The participants were asked to post their comments in the community, but they did not have to write English sentences. All they had to do was to write Japanese sentences as they do in their usual interaction with LINE, and read the English translations the bot automatically generated as seen in Fig. 3.11. The participants were also asked to undergo TOEIC© testing and essay writing before and after the one-month interaction. During the interaction, again Sato did not give the participants any explicit English language instruction.

Experimental Results

The total number of the texts the members posted on the LINE group site on 21 days was 416, as illustrated in Fig. 3.12, whereas there were 533 posts during the previous practice. This means that about 20 posts were submitted per day on average. The maximum number of posts per day was 55 (Day 6), whereas the

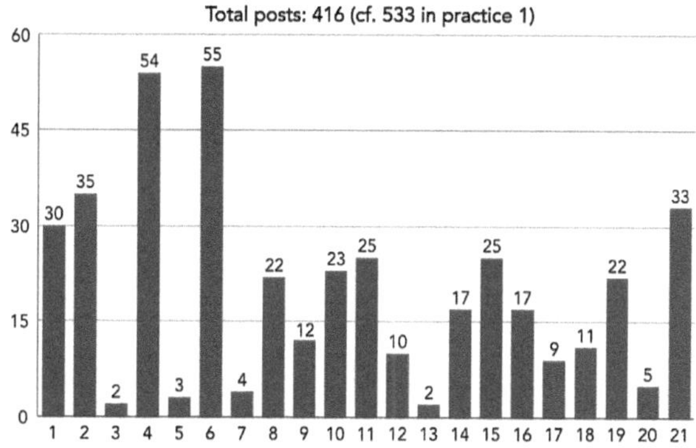

Fig. 3.12 Number of posts to LINE using the Japanese-English translation bot

minimum number was 2 (Day 3 and 13). Although in the previous practice fewer posts were submitted during the last few days, this time the members kept posting texts.

Figure 3.13 shows that the number of English words translated by the bot correlates with the number of the posts per day in the above figure. The total number of English words the bot generated during the period was 5379 (whereas 10,975 English words were posted in the previous practice). This means that 256 English words were generated per day on average. The maximum number of words generated was 720 (on Day 4), whereas the minimum number was 12 (on Day 13).

The number of posts according to the participants is shown in Fig. 3.14. The maximum number of posts one participant submitted was 116 (Member 3), while the minimum number was 19 (Member 6). The average number of posts for this group was 59.4, that is, 2.8 posts per a day during the term.

As for the total English words the translation bot generated from the participants' remarks, shown in Fig. 3.15, the results correlated with Fig. 3.14: Member 3, who posted the most frequently, had 1618 words, while Member 6, who posted the least frequently, had 203 words, which was one-eighth of Member 3's output. The average number of words was 768.4.

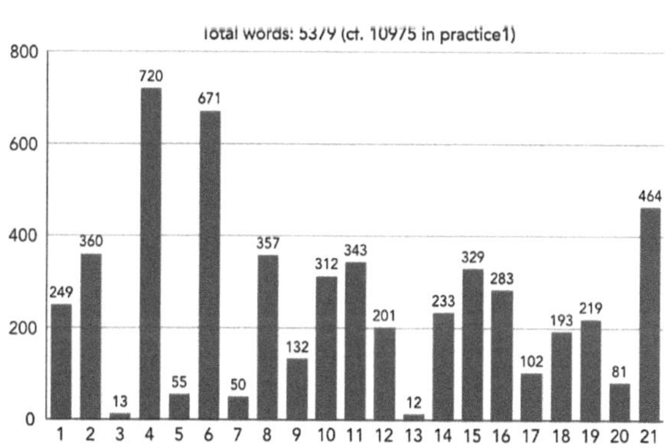

Fig. 3.13 Total English words generated by the translation bot

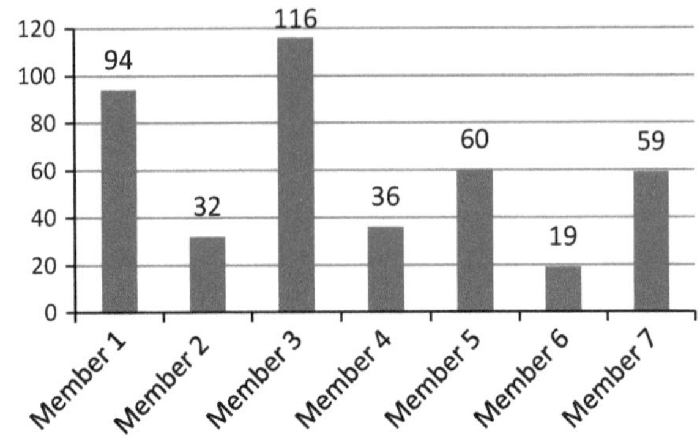

Fig. 3.14 Number of posts by individual members

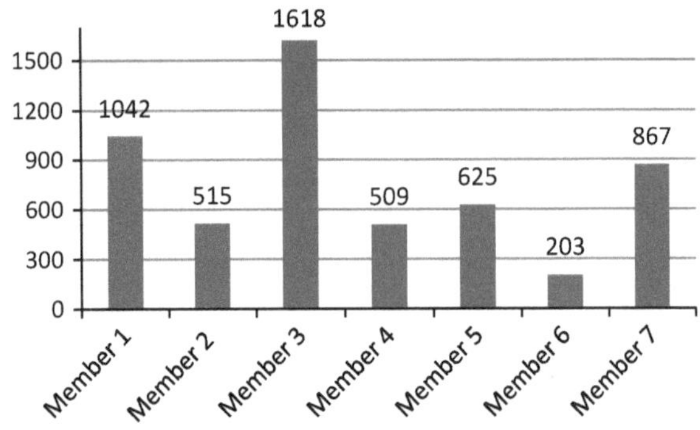

Fig. 3.15 Number of English words generated by the translation bot

Results of TOEIC© tests before and after the interactions are shown in Fig. 3.16. On the whole, the results of the post-test were not improved compared with the previous practice. Among seven participants, three members improved their scores, but four members declined. The average score of their pre-test was 579.3, whereas that of their post-test was 597.1, amounting to an average improvement of 17.9. As for the reading section in the following Fig. 3.17, 4 members improved their scores, but 3 members declined. The average score of their pre-test was 268.6, whereas that

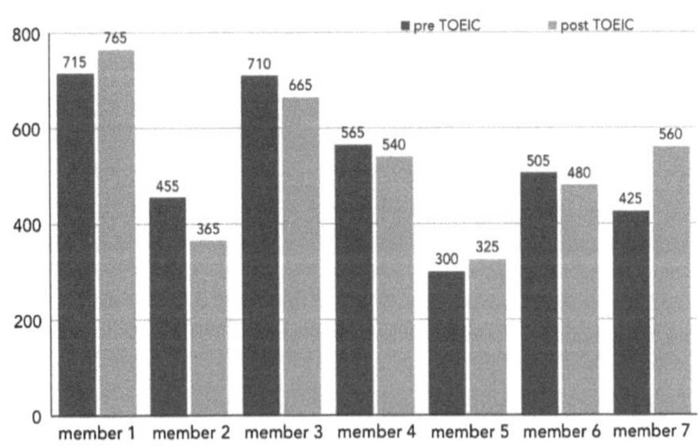

Fig. 3.16 Individual TOEIC© whole test scores

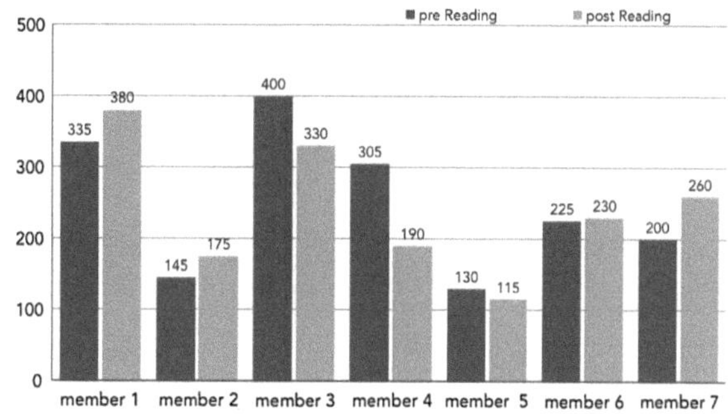

Fig. 3.17 TOEIC© reading scores only

of their post-test was 275.7, amounting to an average improvement of 7.1. Given these results, it can be said that the total scores after the online interaction were modestly higher than before the interaction, indicating that the interaction might have had a slightly positive effect on their English language literacy.

Next, the number of English words the bot generated and the reading section scores of each member are compared. As seen in Fig. 3.18, the results of this practice show less correlation than the previous practice. For instance, the reading score of Member 3, who was most actively engaged in the interaction, decreased from 400 to 330. Meanwhile, Member 2, who participated rather passively in this interaction, improved from 145 to 175. The lack of correlation, however, is not surprising in that the translations were not generated by each member but by the bot; participants posted texts written in Japanese, so it matters not how many words they wrote, but how much of the translations they read, and how correct and meaningful the English was.

As another measure, the essays each member wrote before and after the interaction were analyzed in terms of their readability and average length of a sentence, based on the same presumption as the previous practice that this interaction would give them more exposure to English, resulting in their making longer and more complex sentences. First of all, the readability of each essay was calculated according to ARI. As seen in Fig. 3.19, all essays show improvement in readability

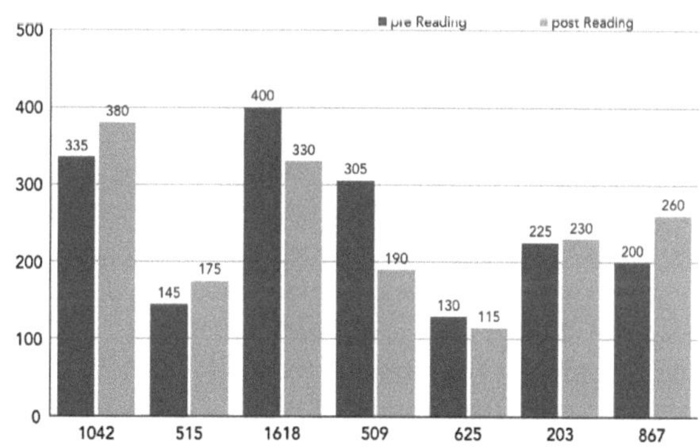

Fig. 3.18 Comparing TOEIC reading scores with total words the bot generated

Fig. 3.19 Readability of the essays

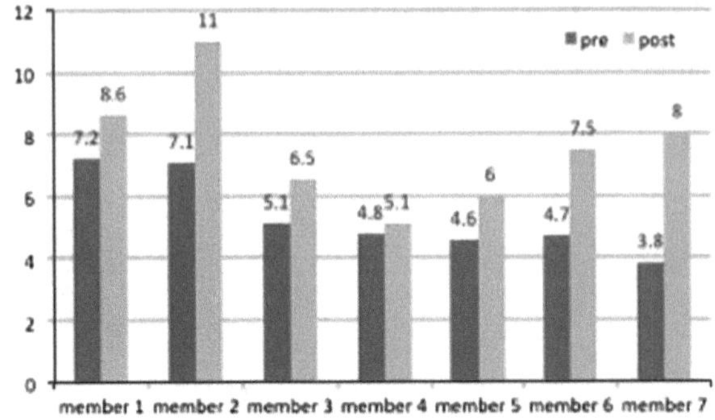

Fig. 3.20 Average length of a sentence

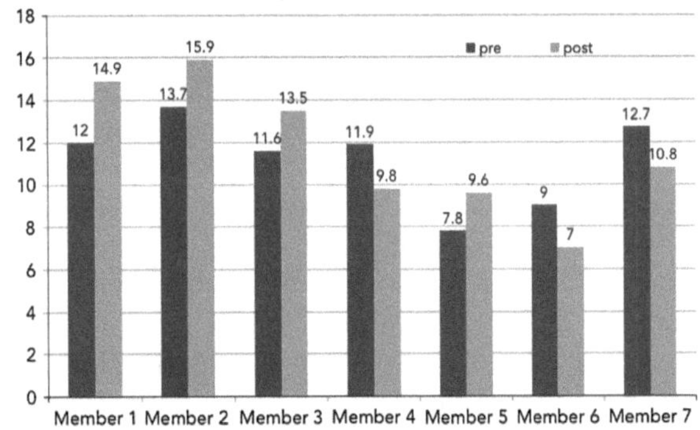

scores. This result indicates that L2 writing skill might be improved by reading English texts the bot automatically generated even though no writing task had been explicitly conducted during the interaction.

However, in terms of the average length of a sentence in their essays shown in Fig. 3.20, four out of seven (Members 1, 2, 3, and 5) increased the number of words per sentence, but three (4, 6 and 7) did not.

Discussion of the Experimental Results

The findings mentioned above illustrate that the interaction with the translation bot in LINE might raise the sophistication of sentences produced, although it may not have a positive impact on the scores of every participant. If so, it could be because the exposure to English expressions the bot generated enhanced their English language competence and, as a result, made it possible to produce more complex sentences despite the fact that no L2 writing task was assigned.

Considering the findings of the two practices, L2 competence could be enhanced not only through the interaction developed in cyberspace, but also through the constant passive exposure to the target language contextualized in their life-worlds. In the first practice, a positive effect was seen in the TOEIC© scores and average length of a sentence, whereas in the second practice the effectiveness was evidenced in the readability scores. Therefore, the use of both approaches, depending on the learners' needs, would constitute one future line of enquiry toward success in mobile-based language learning with the LINE application.

Follow-up Questionnaire Results

Questionnaire research was conducted after all the tasks were completed. All of the questionnaire items and procedures were the same as the first practice.

The first question was the frequency of their checking posts from the other members. Two of the members answered "very often," the other five answered "often."

The second question was the feeling when you submit your post. Three members answered "willingly," and the other four answered "rather willingly."

Then, as for the feeling when you answered questions from the other members, three of them answered "willingly," and the other four answered "rather willingly."

The next inquiry was about their impression of the online interaction they experienced. Five of them answered "enjoyable," one answered "rather enjoyable," and one said it was "rather tough." They were also asked to write the reason they thought so. Here are their responses about this questionnaire item (their comments are translated into English by Sato). Their comments reflect the advantages and disadvantages of the practice:

- I could know something about the members like their hobbies or interests.
- The activity was easy to carry out thanks to LINE.
- Using the translation bot was interesting.
- The activity gave me opportunities to be exposed to English.
- The discussion with the others was more heated than I thought.
- The activity was completely new to me.
- The activity is not a tough one compared with learning English in a classroom.
- I could not read the others' posts because I was busy.

Their comments show that they enjoyed joining the online interaction and it felt less stressful during the interaction with the others than solely English composition might have been without the bot. With the bot they could be exposed to various types of English sentences, all of which were comprehensible together with the Japanese texts. This could mean that the combined input each member got served was strengthened in terms of comprehensible input in the target language (Krashen 1982, 1985), which L2 learners should receive for the improvement of their language competence. Such comprehensible input through the online interaction could account for the improvement of the L2 learners' language competence, as supported by the Interaction Hypothesis (Long 1996).

However, the answers to the final question as to whether this online discussion could become a useful way of L2 learning were not very positive compared with the first practice where all members answered positively. One of them answered "agree" and three "rather agree," while two chose "rather disagree" and one "disagree." The following feedback suggests the reasons they thought so.

- This task offered me a chance to have exposure to English.
- The translation bot lowered my inferiority complex about English.
- I sometimes did not read the English sentences, so the activity was not like learning English.
- I could not write any English sentences but merely read the others' posts.
- The translations the bot showed us were not correct.
- The activity would be useful for reading and writing skills, but not for listening and speaking because all I did was to read posts.

Those comments suggest future challenges for mobile-based language learning with a translation bot. Although they might enjoy interacting with others, they might feel frustrated at the restriction that they could not write any English sentences and they could only read the English translations. This kind of incidental language learning might make the participants less satisfied because the interaction was not like learning specific language targets, even if their L2 competence was improved in some ways.

This type of practice using a translation bot during online interaction might have a positive impact on some learners as when the "translation bot lowered my inferiority complex about English." As L2 writing tasks might be challenging, they might hesitate to write L2 sentences, concerned whether the sentences were grammatically correct or not. They could encounter uncomfortable situations like responses of incomprehension or be asked to rephrase their sentences, as often happens in daily conversation. The translation bot, on the other hand, might scaffold their L2 interaction and lower their anxiety in L2 interaction. In this respect, this practice should be conducted for lower level learners or those who have just started learning a new language.

Recommendations for Other Institutions

MALL might have the potential to resolve issues many learners and teachers have encountered, such as lack of exposure to the target language and inactive learner attitudes. Nearly ubiquitous ownership of mobile devices facilitates easier access to language resources, and an autonomous attitude can be encouraged. The key to success in MALL is not only the ownership of the devices but also the familiarity with mobile functions L2 learners are able to operate for language learning. This familiarity should lower their affective filter in accessing language resources and participating in online discussions with peers, resulting in more L2 input and output than would have occurred solely in the L2 classroom. In the practices here, LINE was chosen as a tool to interact in academic contexts, because it is one of the applications most widely known in Japan for online communication through mobile devices, and its users have familiarized themselves with the basic functions in the process of their daily interactions.

This chapter has introduced two types of practices with LINE. One practice was to interact with the other members by writing English in an online site only for the members developed in LINE. The other was to interact via the translation bot as a function of LINE, which automatically and almost simultaneously translates. The participants only had to write Japanese sentences and read the English translations generated. The results of the TOEIC© tests and the essay writing tasks point to a positive impact of both interactions to an extent. They also illustrate that the more active participants improve their performance more. In addition, the feedback from the participants shows their overall positive attitude toward the practices, while some challenges for a more effective implementation of similar practices were also indicated.

This kind of mobile implementation is easily reproducible and scalable, needing no additional devices, facilities, or administrative assistance. All that is needed is the mobile devices carried by participants and the LINE app (or a similar one commonly used in the reader's region), which is available for various types of mobile devices and PCs free of charge. Taking these findings into account, such conversational tasks with a certain topic via LINE, or other communicative tasks could be implemented as a supplement to classroom-based activities with minimal financial and technical obstacles. Furthermore, LINE does not violate the privacy of users, but the conversation can be conducted under the instructor's supervision by developing private discussion groups of invited students within LINE. In a supportive peer environment, students can be least inhibited from self-expression.

Most of the same principles and considerations would apply to future language learning projects elsewhere utilizing other mobile communication platforms. This study demonstrates that creating expectations of interaction itself motivates the participants, because it offers students the chance to use the target language where there are ordinarily few opportunities to do so in their daily life. In that respect, this practice can be recommended to other educators because it is easily conducted and also useful, in that more exposure to the target language, and more autonomous learning, is facilitated. Whether informally or as part of a class, it is a way of setting up a community of practice with a clear purpose and the means to communicate at a distance anytime and anywhere.

References

Kindai University. (2013, February 8). *Daigakusei no jouhou kiki riyou ni kansuru chousa* [An investigation of college students' ownership of information technology devices]. Retrieved from http://www.kindai.ac.jp/130208.pdf

Krashen, S. (1982). *Principles and practice in second language acquisition*. Oxford: Pergamon.

Krashen, S. (1985). *The input hypothesis*. London: Longman.

Kukulska-Hulme, A., Norris, L., & Donohue, J. (2015). *Mobile pedagogy for English language teaching: a guide for teachers*. London: British Council.

Kukulska-Hulme, A. (2009). Will mobile learning change language learning? *ReCALL, 21*(2), 157–165.

LINE Corporate Announcement. (2016, January 28). LINE corporation announces 2015 fiscal year results. Retrieved from http://linecorp.com/en/pr/news/en/2016/1223

LINE News. (2014, April 2). LINE surpasses 400 million registered users. Retrieved from http://linecorp.com/en/press/2014/0402714

Long, M. H. (1996). The role of the linguistic environment in second language acquisition. In W. C. Ritchie & T. K. Bahtia (Eds.), *Handbook of second language acquisition* (pp. 413–468). New York: Academic Press.

Mainichi Daily News. (2014, October 10). Message app line to seek growth before stock listing: President. Retrieved from http://mainichi.jp/english/english/newsselect/news/20141010p2g00m0bu029000c.html

Ministry of Internal Affairs and Communications of Japan. (2015). *Heisei 26-nen joho tsushin media no riyo jikan to joho kodo ni kan suru chosa* [Research on time spent on IT media and behavior in fiscal year 2014]. Retrieved from http://www.soumu.go.jp/main_content/000357568.pdf

Pachler, N., Bachmair, B., & Cook, J. (2010). *Mobile learning: Structures, agency, practices*. New York: Springer.

Sharples, M., Taylor, J., & Vavoula, G. (2007). A theory of learning for the mobile age. In R. Andrews & C. Haythornthwaite (Eds.), *The Sage handbook of elearning research* (pp. 221–247). London: Sage.

Stockwell, G., & Hubbard, P. (2013). *Some emerging principles for mobile-assisted language learning*. Monterey, CA: The International Research Foundation for English Language Education. Retrieved from http://www.tirfonline.org/english-in-the-workforce/mobile-assisted-language-learning

Swain, M. (2000). The output hypothesis and beyond: Mediating acquisition through collaborative dialogue. In J. Lantolf (Ed.), *Sociocultural approaches to second language research* (pp. 97–115). Oxford: Oxford University Press.

Chapter 4
Osaka Jogakuin University Case Study: Mobilizing the EFL Curriculum and Campus Infrastructure with iPods and iPads

Abstract The second of three case studies in this book covers a combined university and two-year college that have not been deterred by its small size and all-female student body from technological innovations. It was first in the world, a half year before Duke University which usually gets the credit, to give an iPod to all incoming first year students, loaded with faculty-made English listening materials. Then it was among the first, certainly in Japan, to give an iPad to all incoming students, and this time faculty-made e-books were integrated into the curriculum. With campus-wide Wi-Fi, students and teachers could also readily access the Internet in classes. Student focus groups have sharpened annual surveys with quantitative and qualitative feedback to continually refine the pedagogy behind utilizing mobile devices.

Institutional/Pedagogical Context

Historical Background/Pedagogical Aims

Presbyterian missionaries founded a school for girls near Osaka Castle in 1884, which now includes a small liberal arts 2-year college and 4-year university, plus a graduate school. Its pillars are Christianity, human rights, and English education. Only about 1 % of the population of Japan is Christian, but such schools, including Aoyama Gakuin, the next case study, are viewed as highly ethical and trustworthy institutions. With its three pillars noted above, and a mission to raise women who are discerning and active in society, Osaka Jogakuin University (OJU) also works for women's empowerment. In the present age where technology enhances employability and amplifies social action, stereotypes about females are discarded as students are willingly empowered with various information and communication technologies, including mobile learning.

S. McCarty et al., *Implementing Mobile Language Learning Technologies in Japan*, SpringerBriefs in Education, DOI 10.1007/978-981-10-2451-1_4

Sociocultural/Legal Issues Affecting m-Learning/Pedagogy

Women are still striving for social equality as old customs tend to be stronger than legal safeguards. Laws ensuring equal pay for equal work, for example, have not been fully enforced. Discrimination against foreigners is not customary, but laws do not specifically prohibit unequal treatment based on nationality, age, and such categories. On the other hand, when the government moved to protect everyone's personal information privacy, the new law created an obstacle to mobile learning. Teachers do not have the right to know or access private devices of students such as mobile phones. Similar to research on human subjects, students may opt out of mobile learning as part of classes if it involves their private devices, a dilemma that discourages experimentation with blended learning between classes. Even if all students had home computers or smartphones, they could not be incorporated into the curriculum. OJU has solved this problem by giving all incoming students hand-held devices since 2004, as will be seen below, which makes mobile devices an extension of the campus infrastructure.

Profile of Students/Majors/Curriculum

Students all live off campus, attending from mostly Osaka and nearby cities such as Kobe, Nara, and Kyoto. It is in this Kansai region, the western hub of Japan, where OJU is known for its education and care of each student. Its Content-Based English as a Foreign Language curriculum has been recognized by the Ministry of Education (MEXT) as a good practice at both the 2-year and 4-year levels. At the junior college all students major in English, while at the university the first two years are similar, but students specialize in international fields along with English, choosing among communication, business, collaboration (NGO work and the like), or law. The OJU EFL curriculum has been wholly integrated for decades (Swenson et al. 2002; Swenson and Cornwell 2007), which has had the effect of integrating the faculty as well in collaborative pedagogical relationships. The faculty has traditionally included a relatively high percentage of native speakers of English. Thus, many content subjects are taught in English, which makes OJU "immersion-like" (Genesee 2006) or a moderate form of bilingual education. University students also choose a second foreign language (East Asian, European, or Swahili), and junior college students can choose a trilingual course including Korean, while general education at all levels is conducted in Japanese.

Technological Context

Campus IT Infrastructure

OJU has a Learning Solutions Center for IT infrastructure maintenance, student support, supplementary learning materials (such as videos), and faculty support. The faculty member in charge also leads a committee to handle the IT budget and acquisitions, plan government grant proposals, priorities for upgrading infrastructure, and technical training for faculty and management staff. Despite its size, OJU aims for a full range of servers and software learning solutions. Learning management systems have long been used for blended classes, particularly Moodle in recent years, also open source content management systems for updating the school Website, faculty information and online syllabi. The school had been using attendance cards, contrary to the global issues content being taught, so McCarty convinced the IT committee to implement an attendance management system, which includes student records and is accessible online in real time by students or staff. Students touch their ID card like a train pass on a sensor in each classroom. Most recently, Mahara e-Portfolio software is used to preserve student artifacts such as papers, presentations, and videos to show their learning progress. Besides computer labs and study rooms with computers, Wi-Fi is available campus-wide for hand-held devices to access the campus network and the Internet.

Hardware/Devices Available

Besides Windows and Macintosh computers being widely available for classes or independent study, OJU has pioneered mobile learning in the broad sense which includes all hand-held or portable devices. From April 2004, first in the world, all incoming students received an iPod, particularly for mobile language learning. Only when all students have the same devices can the latter serve as an extension of the campus infrastructure for formal assignments and supplemental activities.

Since April 2012, all incoming students have received an iPad, a step much closer than the iPod to ubiquitous learning, since students can access the Internet anywhere on campus via Wi-Fi, albeit only in the homes of some students, or where they can catch Wi-Fi off campus. Now a portable and hand-held device is part of the campus infrastructure, so homework can be assigned utilizing the Web or iPad apps including e-books.

At the same time it is a private matter when students use mobile phones, which nearly all now carry, in addition to, or instead of, their iPad. Their use might be prohibited at times, or negotiated by teachers, but not assumed to be involuntarily available for formal assignments. Particularly with the iPhone, there is an overlap with iPad apps, so students often use their lighter smartphones for functions such as online dictionaries, or taking pictures of the blackboard and other surfaces as a new form of note-taking.

Implementation

Mobile Learning Initiatives/Innovations

Mobile Internet (2000–Present)

Actually three initiatives or phases involving different types of hand-held devices could be detailed here, but technologies still commonly used will be emphasized. The first phase was extra-curricular experimentation with the mobile Internet to motivate EFL students, initiated at a different college in Japan in the year 2000, as described in the last section of the Introduction. Moreover, mobile phones and smartphones have increasingly played an informal learning role in the hands of students in higher education around the world. To summarize the two phases implemented at OJU in Osaka, from 2004–2011 all incoming students received an iPod, particularly for English language listening. 'Podcasting' (explained below) was added as a voluntary activity to enhance integrative motivation. In the most recent phase since 2012, all incoming students have received an iPad, utilized for blended learning through many apps, particularly for faculty-made e-books and accessing the Web through campus-wide Wi-Fi. This phase of portable tablet computing is most replicable by readers, but the second phase may also be instructive, as podcasting is still popular, with sound files easier than ever to access and play on Internet-enabled devices.

iPod/Podcasting (2004–2011)

From April 2004, a half year before Duke University, which is widely credited as first in the world, all OJU incoming students received an iPod, not just the media player but stocked with English listening materials, in order for students to quickly get up to speed for classes with English as the medium of instruction. Homework was assigned in first and second year core courses whereby students would 'synch' their iPod to the iTunes program in Macintosh computers, to copy the English sound files necessary to do their assignments. Teachers and students were also encouraged to find ways to utilize the iPod for other classes and for independent study.

'Podcasts' and other media files could be downloaded from the Web through 'synching' to an iPod. 'Podcasting', a portmanteau of iPod and broadcasting, refers to informally publishing .mp3 format sound files that are then downloaded from blogs or other Websites to the iPod. Like on-demand radio shows, podcasts are preferably syndicated in a series and subscribed to through RSS technology, though RSS is not as widely supported anymore. Podcasting was expanded to 'vodcasting' when iPod models became able to play videos, 'coursecasting' when class lectures were recorded for student review (McCarty 2007), and extended to 'vlogging' when videos were embedded in blogs (McCarty 2010, pp. 100–101, 2011) or available for downloading from other Websites.

Podcasting of audio was suited both to the iPod device and to the 'bandwidth' available at the time, with the capacity to transmit large files rapidly through the Internet still limited for most users in the world. With the popularization of this Apple technology, the iTunes Store began to review and accept the streams of some podcasters in a separate category from music, either for a price or free. A Web-based ecology of sites hosting, supporting, listing and reviewing podcasts thus grew for several years.

With the iPod in the hands of OJU students, McCarty started recording podcasts, either with a microphone connected to a computer or on the go with a hand-held MP3 voice recorder, later connected to the computer through a USB port. The small voice recorder was convenient for recording conference presentations and making them available later on the open Web for listening while viewing the PowerPoint slides. Podcasts were posted with descriptions under the title 'Japancasting' at a podcasting blog hosting site in Canada, and free for subscribers also at the iTunes Store.

Podcasts were in English or Japanese, of interest both to EFL students and those interested in Japan or Japanese. Various topics included the author's research and commentary on Japan, interviews with Japanese professors, academic presentations, the lecture part of EFL classes (coursecasting), interviews with students, and performances of student-generated content. During a translation practicum taught at another university, a trilingual podcast was recorded in Japanese, Chinese, and English, with students discussing proverbs in their cultures that have the same meaning as English ones. OJU students were invited to publish their performances in campus English speaking contests. Podcasting at OJU was described as a case of Web 2.0 pedagogy: "Students contribute to the professor's bilingual podcast feed and blog—targeted to those studying Japanese or English as a second language—by being interviewed by their professor, performing roles, or presenting their own creations" (McLoughlin and Lee 2008).

Though it took extra time outside of class to record podcasts, the students were pleased to reach a global audience and receive positive feedback, which enhanced their integrative motivation (McCarty 2009a; defined by Gardner, cited in McCarty 2010, p. 88). The target language community becomes more approachable, while a more personal relationship with the teacher is motivating to students (Dörnyei 2001, pp. 31–39). Another way to enhance integrative motivation is to reach students where they are active outside of class by social networking (McCarty 2009b).

One essential theoretical support for student-generated content is that learners can "experience new identities as authors, narrators, interpreters and critics through their second language" (Williams and Burden 1997, p. 22). Rather than passive spectators of the English speaking world, students were actually engaged in its discourse as content creators. The Japancasting site was thus featured in magazines in Japan, rated highly in many podcasting repositories abroad, and the podcasting of student-generated content was designated an "effective practice" by the Online Learning Consortium (2007) based in the U.S.

After several years, however, the podcast hosting sites suddenly went offline with the advent of YouTube, Twitter, and other user-friendly social networking sites. At the same time the Internet infrastructure including for mobile phones grew in the bandwidth needed to transmit multimedia files directly online. Japancasting podcasts are now available to download individually along with YouTube videos, presentations, and publications at www.waoe.org/steve/epublist.html.

Since the iPod was actually used offline, even if the files originated online, the iPod represented an intermediate stage on the way to direct mobile Internet access to multimedia, what McCarty (2005) called "spoken Internet to go". The technology at that stage was awkward to use, whereas ease of use or, more generally, usability is an important criterion for adoption and sustained use of technologies (cf., e.g., Kujala and Miron-Shatz 2013). Thus, the demand for user-friendly, high-bandwidth, direct access to multimedia through the Internet eventually led to new generations of technologies superseding dedicated media players like the iPod. The rest of this chapter will therefore focus on the current phase.

iPad/e-Books (2012–Present)

In April 2012, OJU became "the first university in Japan to provide all incoming students with an iPad" (Swenson et al. 2013, p. 20). A portable and Internet-capable device is now part of the campus infrastructure for in-class activities, homework, and ubiquitous learning to some extent. An iPad can contain "an eBook library, a digital camera and video camera, a recorder, a computer" and one can "send email, or have live conversations via messaging applications, watch videos, listen to lectures and conversations, give presentations and access news stories" (Bramley 2014, p. 90).

As with the iPod, OJU is an early adopter of the iPad, encouraging students to take advantage of its affordances and acquire recommended apps for study support, while encouraging teachers to find new apps and uses for the iPad in and between classes. The iPad is incorporated into the curriculum first of all through courses using e-books as textbooks, while much paper is saved by publishing the formerly bulky student handbooks only electronically. Students are directed to download faculty-created e-books from a certain URL on campus servers, usually logging into the Moodle LMS with their student ID and their own password. Currently some second year listening courses use commercial e-books, which is likely to be a more common practice than in-house creation using iBooks Author or other such programs. For those courses, students pay and download the e-books, while teachers can download other materials as well, such as transcripts and quizzes (Sarosy and Sherak 2013). Classes are generally taught by connecting the teacher's iPad to the projector and sound system that is in nearly every classroom at OJU.

Playing a more essential role in the OJU curriculum is the array of faculty-created e-books used in all of the first year core English courses. The core courses are designed to cover the four skills, with reading and writing exercises, and listening incorporated into topic discussion classes. Content-based EFL textbooks on global issues developed by the faculty over many years were turned into e-books, but adding new material and interactive affordances built with the iBooks Author program. Certain content areas have been designated as parts of the integrated curriculum, thus the e-books for reading and discussion in particular focus on specific topics in global issues such as conflict and peacemaking, values and ethics, human rights, and a sustainable future.

Swenson et al. (2013) detail how the first nine e-books were made, not just copying texts and pasting them into e-book form but rather taking advantage of the interactivity that can be built into e-books with iBooks Author. While Apple's program is exclusively for iPad e-books and freely available only on Macintosh computers at present, there are other e-book making programs for various formats such as the open source EPUB available at http://idpf.org/epub. Features of OJU e-books include color photo collections for discussion, which would be prohibitively expensive in paper textbooks, while of course a tablet is much lighter to carry. More importantly, interactive functions not available in regular textbooks include hyperlinks to Websites, which, after clicking, open the Safari Web browsing program to that URL and hide the e-book in the background. Other interactive functions utilized at OJU include self-check quizzes for vocabulary or comprehension, highlighting, and notes typed by students into the e-book in designated places. Notations are automatically compiled at the back of the e-book, and homework can be emailed to the teacher from within the e-book. Oxford University Press has its own set of tools including voice notes that can be placed anywhere in their e-books (Sarosy and Sherak 2013). The teacher can also record selected parts of the text and click to play the audio over the room speakers (Fig. 4.1).

The iBooks Author program features widgets inserted into e-books to make them interactive. Besides the functions discussed above, namely the Gallery widget for photos with captions, and Review for multiple-choice or drag-to-target questions, other useful widgets are Media for inserting videos and sound files, Keynote for presentation files, and Pop-Over for text boxes or images that are clicked to pop open over an e-book page, for example temporarily showing a definition or a script of spoken media. Also available is a 3D widget to make images able to be rotated and Scrolling Sidebar for optional supplementary information that would not otherwise fit on the page. There is also an HTML5 widget for professional developers. Many other widgets, including for games and puzzles, can be downloaded from sites like http://bookry.com (Swenson et al. 2013, pp. 22–24).

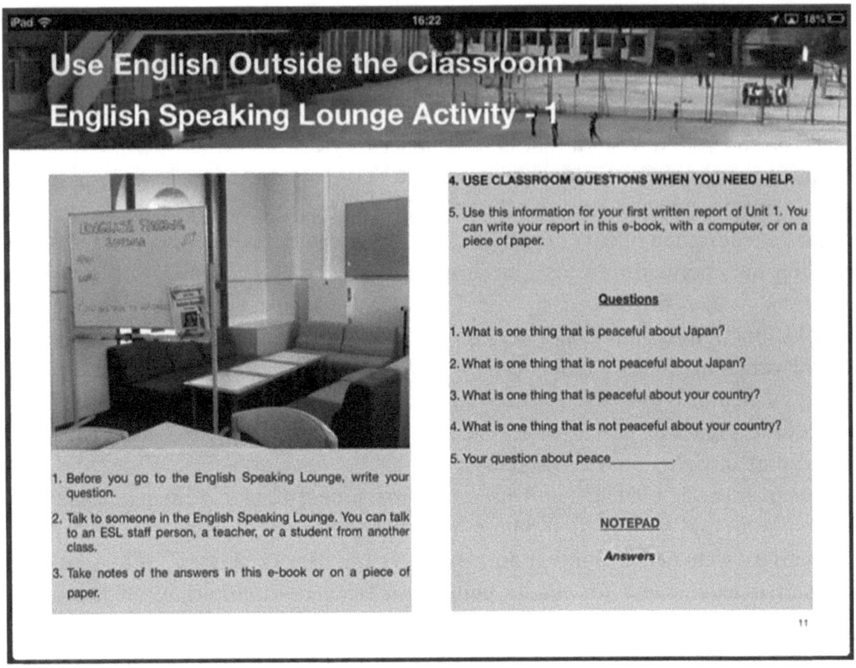

Fig. 4.1 OJU first year e-book assignment to speak English outside of class

Faculty/Staff/Student Training

The making of e-books with iPad Author has been a time-consuming effort by several long-time faculty members, with specific tasks delegated to others. Particularly teachers who use the iPad in class for e-books may borrow an iPad from the school or order one with research funds. Students receive an iPad on their day of entrance, with a video introduction to the iPad during the ceremony, by a second year student in 2014. During the orientation week there are sessions for students to learn about the iPad and campus IT infrastructure including computers. There are also occasional training sessions offered, one where "Big Sisters" who have gone through the first year offer advice to first year students who attend voluntarily.

With the vast array of hardware and software in use, there is also a first year course in IT that helps familiarize students with learning technologies. They will, for example, take surveys to evaluate most classes online via iPad or computer, which in turn saves labor and paper, as the results are automatically compiled.

The Learning Solutions Center (LSC) helps the students individually in various ways, offering listening media or troubleshooting, and also supports teachers using technology in class. As another example, the LSC recommends certain iPad apps, free to download, for study support.

The LSC is guided by a faculty and staff IT committee, which for example seeks government grants to upgrade the infrastructure. There have been occasional faculty and staff training sessions each semester over the years, but it can never be long enough or frequent enough in busy schedules to serve everyone's needs with so many technologies in use. Bramley alludes to a gap between full-time faculty and part-time instructors in having students use iPad and e-book functions, which is partly due to the difference in technical training offered (2015).

The occasional formal technical training sessions are mostly in Japanese, to serve the majority of faculty and staff, while the technical staff members have limited English proficiency. Both for presenters and recipients of technology support, or reading user manuals independently, learning new technologies is more difficult in one's second language.

Administrative/Stakeholder Cooperation/Challenges

Some intrinsic challenges have already been mentioned with an international faculty and a rapidly changing technological landscape. Then there is also the variety of stakeholders with a wide range of understanding and attitudes toward the use of technologies to support learning. For campus-wide systems to appear in the first place, cooperation from the top decision-makers is necessary. In the case of OJU there is a consensus welcoming whatever technologies empower learners, while the students themselves find the mobile devices fashionable as well as useful. All universities have administrators and faculty members who do not keep up with technological advances, while a number of students would rather not be bothered by the required use of certain devices and online sites. For example, students can set their campus email account to automatically forward messages to their mobile phone. Perfect communication is an elusive goal. However, most OJU students are eager to use online and mobile technologies for the sake of convenience, effective study, employability, and empowerment in contemporary society.

There will always be challenges in implementing technologies, and limitations such as economic costs of adoption, or usability issues such as the small screens of mobile devices. At the same time, new technologies present a positive challenge to use them to extend the reach of the university into the local community and the world (McCarty 2010, pp. 89–90). Stakeholders include everyone on campus, while online technologies make it possible to serve other stakeholders including parents of students (McCarty 2011), alumni, and high school students who may be interested in the university (McCarty 2010, pp. 97–100).

Assessment of Effectiveness

Regarding the effectiveness of the mobile devices implemented for language learning at OJU, as noted earlier, podcasts to leverage students' iPods were highly evaluated internationally by many curating sites and academic repositories, and the podcasting of student-generated EFL content was assessed as an "effective practice" (Online Learning Consortium 2007). Years of questionnaire results also led to the confidence that introducing the iPad into the curriculum before other universities in Japan would also be successful for learning outcomes.

Regarding the response of students to using the iPad and e-books, early focus groups, recent questionnaires, and discussions with individual students present a mostly positive picture. However, some of the same issues with paper materials still remain, such as the level of materials or the cognitive load of assignments relative to the various English levels of students. A commercial series of e-books (Sarosy and Sherak 2013) seemed to teachers to be a more interesting approach to academic listening, yet intermediate level second year students found the long and realistic university lectures on video and audio too difficult to understand. Some of the in-house e-book materials on global issues were also found to be difficult for lower level first year students. Regardless of the technology, teachers must find the right level of the language to start from the students' level of readiness.

Looking over student comments in Japanese on a questionnaire about the iPad and e-books, it seems remarkable how quickly they take new technologies for granted. While students showed appreciation for e-books as compared with carrying heavy textbooks, some students found the iPad Mini heavy, which probably means that their point of comparison is their smartphone. There are also students who find the print too small on the iPad Mini, or would prefer regular textbooks without having to deal with the technology. While some students may prefer to use the same apps as their iPad on their iPhone, the typeface is even smaller, yet students are used to it, since Japan's ICT culture has centered on mobile phones (*keitai*) since the 1990s. Isolated comments or limited data can present a confusing picture, so it is important to compile complete and longitudinal survey results.

Bramley (2014) summarizes the responses of a focus group of 20 OJU students who were asked questions about the iPad and e-books. Students found the iPad convenient for learning and for carrying textbooks easily. Their favorite iPad functions were games, YouTube videos and other movies, music, and photos. They disliked the short battery life, with the power sometimes going off in class or in the midst of activities. Some students with the larger iPad 2 found it heavy, while others found the small screen of the iPad Mini a disadvantage (pp. 103–104).

The focus group reported using their iPad for homework, with dictionaries and other study support apps, for making presentations, and for listening exercises in their e-books. There were also students who had not used their iPad or e-books yet. Features of the e-books made by the OJU faculty that were liked by students included picture galleries, which were easy to understand and good for speaking; audio files, good for listening and improving their pronunciation; and (self-checking) review quizzes. They found the note-taking and highlighting functions useful, such as for making electronic vocabulary cards or highlighting features of readings such as topic sentences or transitions (Bramley 2014, pp. 104–105).

The above focus group responses informed the construction of a more detailed survey in 2014. Among the results, most frequent use of the iPad was for looking up words in dictionaries and for translation outside of class. First year students more often submitted homework than second year students, since first year classes use e-books with such assignments. Other uses of the iPad, in class more than occasionally, in order of average frequency were: to take photos, take notes, download apps or materials, do research on the Web, make presentations, read for fun, and watch or take videos. They also occasionally did social networking on their iPad and emailed teachers or fellow students. Out of class, the results differed mainly in students watching videos, reading for pleasure or research, and social networking more often. Students rarely purchased apps but often downloaded free apps for, in order of frequency, English study, games, photography, productivity, social networking, and searching the Web. Bramley also noted that many students prefer to use their smartphone outside of class for some of the same basic tasks (2015, pp. 34–36).

Written comments on the survey form showed mostly positive attitudes toward iPad use. Students find it easy to carry and turn in homework by email, while it holds many e-books and offers many possible functions. One limitation is screen size for reading, especially with the iPad Mini. Moreover, e-books made by iPad Author do not yet allow for the function of enlarging page sections by fingers and thumb. Models with 16 GB of memory can fill up quickly with e-books so that earlier ones have to be deleted. Battery life is also a problem when students become unable to use their iPad in class (Bramley 2015, p. 37).

The data show that students generally understand the common uses of the iPad, better than some teachers, which emboldens faculty members to develop further uses and materials for the platform.

Recommendations for Other Institutions

In many countries today, teachers see nearly all students holding mobile phones or other portable devices. World Bank (2014) data add up to more cell phone subscriptions per year than people in the world, with an average of more than two per person in Macao and Hong Kong. Mobile devices therefore present a tantalizing target to exploit for learning languages and other subjects. Yet many limitations become apparent when students have different devices of their own. Under Japan's personal privacy laws, mobile exercises can only be voluntary, and there is a strong expectation of equal access to learning opportunities for every student in a class. Even if teachers in other countries can ask for students' personal addresses to communicate assignments or supplementary activities, challenges remain in the diversity and frequent changes in the devices students use.

The OJU experience shows that maximum use is possible when all students are given the same devices, then the devices can be incorporated into the curriculum as an extension of the campus infrastructure. Students' tuition indirectly pays for the devices in that case, while government grants or research funds can be sought for devices to hand out to all students in a class temporarily.

Another lesson from the OJU experience is to be an early adopter of technologies at the individual and institutional levels. A spirit of experimentation without fear of technologies and the unknown will certainly result in greater technological competence, while it may also result in greater recognition for the university in a society with competing educational institutions. As there are no shortcuts in a world of rapidly changing technologies, class experiments and broader implementations accumulate expertise in the institution. Each effort adds readiness to mount the next innovation.

Certain waves of technology use will sweep across the world whether a given university is a leader, imitator, or not on board, in which case tech-savvy students may have less respect for what the curriculum or professoriate offers. The waves of technology can be sudden and unexpected, and some may turn out to be temporary fads, so institutions need to exercise discernment in choosing or developing new technologies. There are certain indicators and long-term trends that can be watched to help judge which technologies to adopt, such as increasing ease of use and capacity of networks to transmit data. In 2004 it was possible to introduce the iPod at OJU, and podcasting also popularized the sharing of sound files (McCarty 2005). Scenic video of McCarty speaking was available for download from the Web from early 1998, but it was the era of the 'world wide wait', especially for heavy files. After sound files peaked in popularity, increasing bandwidth and compression of movie files into Flash format allowed for the popularization of YouTube and other forms of online video. By 2012, with years of iPod experience and a more robust global Internet infrastructure, OJU was ready to utilize the iPad as a portable computer that could take photos, videos, and so forth, while accessing the Internet via Wi-Fi. In contrast with heavy video cameras, related equipment and other challenges of making online videos until recently (McCarty 2011), now the free YouTube Capture app can be recommended for taking, trimming, and combining videos, then uploading them to social media like YouTube, Facebook, and Twitter, all from within the iPad.

An often neglected criterion for sustainability of technologies is how well they can serve universal human needs. Social media and social networking sites have broadened the reach of interpersonal relationships, yet they are usually described in terms of social software rather than how they simulate and expand upon face-to-face relationships to fulfill innate social aspirations. Technologies perceived as enhancing access to new social as well as learning opportunities will be welcomed on campus.

References

Bramley, D. (2014). Tap into the future: A study of iPads and interactive eBooks in an e-learning project. *Osaka JALT Journal, 1*(1), 89–108. Retrieved from http://www.osakajalt.org/storage/journal/Osaka%20JALT%20Journal%20March%202014.pdf

Bramley, D. (2015). Tablet computers and eBooks: Student feedback. *Journal of Osaka Jogakuin University, 11*, 23–43.

Dörnyei, Z. (2001). *Motivational strategies in the language classroom*. Cambridge, UK: Cambridge University Press.

Genesee, F. (2006, June 12). *Content-based foreign language instruction: Models and methods*. Lecture presented at Kansai University, Osaka, Japan.

Kujala, S., & Miron-Shatz, T. (2013). Emotions, experiences and usability in real-life mobile phone use. In W. E. Mackay et al. (Eds.), *CHI'13 Proceedings of the SIGCHI Conference on Human Factors in Computing Systems* (pp. 1061–1070). New York: ACM.

McCarty, S. (2005). Spoken internet to go: Popularization through podcasting. *JALT CALL Journal, 1*(2), 67–74.

McCarty, S. (2007). Window into the classroom: Podcasting an english for professional purposes course. *Osaka Jogakuin Junior College Journal, 36*, 1–21.

McCarty, S. (2009a). Curtain CALL: Online performances for integrative motivation. In M. Thomas (Ed.), *New frontiers in CALL: Negotiating diversity* (pp. 71–76). Tokyo: JALT CALL SIG.

McCarty, S. (2009b). Social networking behind student lines in Japan. In M. Thomas (Ed.), *Handbook of research on web 2.0 and second language learning* (pp. 181–201). Hershey, PA: IGI Global.

McCarty, S. (2010). Social media to motivate language learners from before admission to after graduation. In W. M. Chan, et al. (Eds.), *Media in foreign language teaching and learning* (pp. 87–105). Centre for Language Studies: National University of Singapore.

McCarty, S. (2011). Vlogging abroad: YouTube reports from New Zealand to Japan. *EduTech: e-Journal of Education & Technology* (September 2011 issue, Indira Gandhi National Open University, New Delhi).

McLoughlin, C., & Lee, M. J. W. (2008). Future learning landscapes: Transforming pedagogy through social software. *Innovate: Journal of Online Education, 4*(5).

Online Learning Consortium (2007). Podcasting student performances to develop EFL skills. Effective Practices—Student-Generated Content. Retrieved from http://onlinelearningconsortium.org/effective_practices/podcasting-student-performances-develop-efl-skills

Sarosy, P. & Sherak, K. (2013). *Lecture ready 1: Strategies for academic listening and speaking*. Oxford: Oxford University Press (textbook, Website & e-book).

Swenson, T., Bramley, D., & Cornwell, S. (2013). Making interactive eBooks: More than just cutting and pasting. *Journal of Osaka Jogakuin University, 10*, 17–30.

Swenson, T., Chihara, T., & McKay, T. (2002). Integrating courses across the curriculum. *Osaka Jogakuin Junior College Journal, 31*, 1–12.

Swenson, T., & Cornwell, S. (2007). Pulling a curriculum together: Addressing content and skills across English and Japanese. In M. Carroll (Ed.), *Developing a new curriculum for adult learners* (pp. 107–129). Washington, D.C.: TESOL.

Williams, M., & Burden, R. (1997). *Psychology for language teachers: A social-constructivist approach*. Cambridge, UK: Cambridge University Press.

World Bank (2014). Mobile cellular subscriptions (per 100 people). Indicators. The Data Catalog. Retrieved from http://data.worldbank.org/indicator/

Chapter 5
Aoyama Gakuin University Case Study: Blended Learning and Flipped Classrooms Utilizing Mobile Devices

Abstract The third and last case study examines blended and flipped classrooms utilizing mobile devices in teaching EFL in Japan. M-Learning can offer a rich, motivating, informal, contextual, and ubiquitous learning environment, where students control their learning time, environment, and pace. Third-year economics majors were given iPads, with e-books integrated into the curriculum. Three empirical studies examined the effectiveness of blended and flipped learning with various emerging technologies from voice recognition to Web-based applications accessed by iPads and smartphones. Results of computer assessment tests such as the CASEC, OPIc speaking test, and TOEIC indicated that blended and flipped lessons helped students to improve their overall English proficiency better than traditional approaches.

Institutional/Pedagogical Context

Historical Background/Pedagogical Aims

Aoyama Gakuin University (AGU) is a Japanese Christian university in Shibuya Ward, Tokyo. AGU is part of Aoyama Gakuin, which includes a kindergarten, an elementary school, junior and senior high schools, and a women's junior college. It was founded in 1874 by Methodist Episcopal missionaries from the United States. Higher education began in 1949 when Aoyama Gakuin College was established. Today, AGU is one of the most prestigious private universities in Japan. It is active in international exchange programs for students and faculty. Few universities in Japan are known for having such a cosmopolitan atmosphere as well as a prized location, with its main campus in a fashionable and trend-setting district of Tokyo. AGU is a mission school with a pedagogical focus mainly on liberal arts education.

S. McCarty et al., *Implementing Mobile Language Learning Technologies in Japan*, SpringerBriefs in Education, DOI 10.1007/978-981-10-2451-1_5

Profile of Students/Majors/Curriculum

Students all live off campus, attending mostly from Tokyo and its surrounding prefectures. Besides the main campus in central Tokyo, the Sagamihara Campus in Kanagawa Prefecture is where freshmen and sophomores study, and a College of Science and Engineering is also located there. The total undergraduate student population at AGU is about 20,000, with about 1300 full-time faculty members and part-time teachers. Undergraduate and graduate programs include literature, law, economics, and business; international majors such as politics, economics, and communication; science, engineering, cultural and creative studies, among others. Graduate programs also include professional training in international management, accounting, a law school, and other specializations.

Technological Context

Campus IT Infrastructure

AGU has a Foreign Language Laboratory for IT infrastructure maintenance, student support, supplementary learning materials (such as videos), and faculty support. The faculty member in charge also leads a committee to handle the IT budget and acquisitions, priorities for upgrading infrastructure, and technical training for faculty and management staff. AGU aims for a full range of servers and software learning solutions. The CHIeru learning management system (LMS) and Courser Power LMS have long been used for blended classes, also open source content management systems for providing various teaching materials including BBC news. AGU has 16 fully equipped language laboratories at the Shibuya (Tokyo) campus, and six open learning laboratories at the Sagamihara campus to support foreign language learning.

Furthermore, AGU has been using the LMS Cyber Campus System (CCS) since 2010 to promote e-Learning and m-Learning. The AGU Human Innovation Research Center (HIRC) is now playing an important role in many projects in this field. The HIRC mobile learning project has published many articles related to e-Learning and m-Learning in the field of English language teaching and has had a great impact at AGU on the pedagogy of EFL teaching methods.

Hardware/Devices Available

Besides Windows and Macintosh computers being widely available for classes or independent study, AGU has pioneered mobile learning in the broad sense that includes all handheld or portable devices. From April 2003, several projects have been conducted toward the integration of e-Learning and m-Learning to enhance language learning. The CHIeru, CaLabo EX, and CALL system, widely used in Japan, has served as the main platform for these initiatives to help students learn foreign languages more efficiently by integrating mobile technologies.

Nearly, 100 % of students are now using smartphones and, as of this wring, 30 % of students are using tablets for learning English. Among 45 students in Obari's seminar class, all of them utilized iPads and smartphones in order to learn English and international affairs. In 2014, students started subscribing to the Asahi Digital Newspaper for language learning and social studies.

Most of the students are very familiar with making digital storytelling projects and PowerPoint presentations, while using partly online e-books as textbooks, such as Oxford *Lecture Ready 1* and *2* (Sarosy and Sherak 2013a, b). Students are highly engaged in active learning and project-based learning with iPads.

Implementation

Blended Learning and Flipped Classrooms Utilizing Mobile Devices

Theoretical Considerations

Mobile learning technologies are rapidly gaining popularity around the world as an effective way to enhance foreign language education. Mobile (m)-Learning is highly motivating to learners, as it offers them a rich, informal, contextual, and ubiquitous learning environment in which it is possible for them to control their learning time, environment, and speed (space and pace). M-Learning has other advantages over conventional teaching and learning methods, including the almost limitless number of English news programs, language learning apps, podcasting (audio series), vodcasting (video shows), and so forth, that can be easily accessible and downloadable for free or for little cost. Today, mobile devices are omnipresent. Recent innovations in technology that brought the advent of social media, such as Facebook and Twitter, to such popularity can be experienced smoothly with handheld devices. Voice over Internet Protocol (VOIP) technology is no longer tied to the desktop or laptop computer. Credit card purchases and other transactions are now commonly performed with mobile devices. However, what is being used so easily and by so many today in society can it be altered, borrowed, copied, or transformed to serve as an effective tool in an educational setting? That is one question addressed in this chapter.

In the field of second language learning (L2), and in computer-assisted language learning (CALL) in particular, there has been an increasing body of research dedicated to the use of mobile devices in language learning in recent years. More technologically oriented teachers and researchers use the term mobile-assisted language learning (MALL) readily as an extension of CALL, as if the term is familiar to everyone in the L2 field. Regarding the roots of MALL and its place in language learning, see Stockwell (2012b) for a detailed discussion. Our purpose here as educators is rather to try and determine whether mobile-assisted learning holds benefits for our students, to see how and why students come to use this technology, and how mobile learning compares with more traditional classroom approaches.

Gardner (2007), in a study pertaining to language learning in Spain, revisits his construct of the socio-educational model first proposed in 1985, which emphasizes integrativeness—how well a student wants to interact with members of another culture—and his or her attitude toward a learning situation as being the keys to successful language learning. Ryan and Deci (2000) return to their earlier Self-Determination Theory and further theorize on motivations, intrinsic and extrinsic, claiming that autonomy plays a large role in the former, while with extrinsic motivation, attitudes toward the teacher, methodology, and the learning environment are factors that promote or inhibit motivation. Further, they assert that, over time, intrinsic motivation fades, while internalization and integration of values and regulation of behaviors in extrinsically motivated learners lead to successful language learning.

Dörnyei (2010) weighs in with his own ideas on the role of motivation in language learning when he proposes the concept of the Ideal Self. Here he suggests that integrativeness, as proposed by Gardner (see above), be reinterpreted, and he provides the results of empirical studies in Hungary as justification. Furthermore, he claims that the traditional theory of instrumental motivation should be rethought and suggests that a learner's attitude to the L2 learning environment be considered as another key factor in determining motivation. As can be seen here, there has been a merger (or at least a meeting) of distinct disciplines, second language learning theory and psychology. But, Dörnyei (2009) takes this one step further when he brings evidence to bear from neuropsychological research, which would take extra study for most language teachers to confirm the new findings that emerge.

The final area of study that will be addressed here is perceptions of learning. Much has been written about how CALL stacks up with more traditional classroom approaches; see in particular Levy (1997) and Stockwell (2012a), both of whom give exhaustive coverage to this important area but in different eras. The literature on learning using mobile devices and student reactions—other than criticism as it pertains to the devices' limitations, size and thus readability (see Chinnery 2006)—is still rather limited, as publications to date tend to describe the types of devices used, e.g., PDAs, cell phones, etc., and outcomes expected. See Kukulska-Hulme and Shield (2008) for an investigation into collaborative learning regarding listening and speaking activities, and Stockwell (2008) for a study focusing on vocabulary. One earlier study of interest regarding types of activities on various mobile devices and student reaction perceptions can be found in Thornton and Houser (2005). Fujimoto (2013) recently reported on Australian students' mobile device ownership and usage patterns, while Miangah and Nezarat (2012) report on employing mobile devices in Iran as a means of cutting costs and overcoming immobile limitations of CALL.

e-Mobile or m-Learning technologies such as the iPhone or iPad, with Internet affordances such as podcasting, videocasting, and more, are rapidly gaining popularity as an effective means to improve foreign language skills around the world. Mobile learning is highly motivating to learners, as it offers them a rich, informal, contextual, and ubiquitous learning environment. Users can control the time, pace, and speed of their own learning, which is motivating and liberating for many learners. M-Learning can also be more personalized than other methods of computerized instruction, as mobile devices can be more easily customized, resulting in the creation of an emotional bond between the user and machine (Sherimon et al. 2011).

M-Learning has indeed emerged as the next generation of e-Learning. One of the reasons for this has been the high availability of mobile devices worldwide. For example, nearly 100 % of Japanese own a mobile phone, with the number of smartphone users in Japan rapidly increasing (Obari et al. 2010). The smaller screen size and touch interface of smartphones and tablets also lead to more focused learning, as the learner typically has running in the background just a single program at any given time, as opposed to the more common multitasking operations found on desktop and notebook PCs (Gualtieri 2011).

The use of mobile technologies for language learning has numerous advantages over other methods, for example, the countless number of English news programs, language learning apps, podcasts, and videos that are easily accessible and free or reasonably priced. Web-based resources using Web 2.0 tools and mobile computing technologies can be integrated to promote collaborative learning activities.

Blended Learning

According to Vinu et al. (2011), mobile technologies have succeeded in transforming learning methodologies. One such methodology that has received great attention in recent years is blended learning (BL). BL combines traditional face-to-face classroom methods with computer-mediated activities, resulting in a more integrated approach for both instructors and learners (Singh and Reed 2001).

(1) Blended learning (BL) prevents learner isolation and reduces the number of dropouts.
(2) Stanford University has reported success in raising students' self-paced course completion rate from a little over 50–94 % by incorporating the elements of BL through the scheduling of live events, facilitating interaction between instructors and peers, and providing mentoring experiences (Singh and Reed 2001).
(3) A blended learning best practice survey conducted by the eLearning Guild (2003) revealed that 73.6 % of respondents reported BL to be more effective than non-blended approaches (as quoted in Wilson and Smilanich 2005, p. 15).

Blended learning (BL) can increase the options for greater quality and quantity of interaction in a learning environment. Mobile devices and social media are a key to the next generation of educational instruction. Digital content has been experiencing a great transformation in its form and volume as mobile technologies and social media continue to spread widely. The Internet has become a vast potential learning platform in itself. By accessing digital contents or through connecting with other people through the Internet, users can acquire deeper as well as wider knowledge about various subjects.

Social learning, a style of learning reinvigorated by social media, is expected to be afford many new applications to learning through the Internet, particularly as the word can spread rapidly about Open Educational Resources (OER). Social learning makes it possible to share insights and connect the knowledge of all learners in an online community. OpenCourseWare (OCW) can also provide more accessible platforms for learning communities. Social learning (Bandura 1977) connects learners with other learners, which can now be accomplished effectively through social media and mobile devices such as smartphones and tablet PCs.

Having a consistently available time and place for learning, particularly where classmates can socialize and receive encouragement, advice, and feedback from a knowledgeable teacher, fulfills important conditions for learning, by building self-confidence and motivation. According to social constructionism, people create new knowledge and learn most effectively through social interaction and exchanging information for mutual benefit. Constructionism also holds that learning can happen most effectively when people are active in making tangible objects in the real world. In this sense, constructionism is connected with experiential learning and builds upon the ideas of Jean Piaget (Burr 1995, 2003).

Mobile Learning Initiatives/Innovations

The goal of this chapter is to show the effectiveness of blended learning and flipped classroom activities using mobile devices for the purpose of improving the English language proficiency of Japanese undergraduates, including their writing, oral communication, presentation skills, and improvements in TOEIC scores. First, the blended learning technologies, activities, and assessments are presented, so the Method Section refers just to the blended learning experiments. After discussing the different assessments of the blended learning results, two flipped classroom projects are summarized. Since flipped classrooms are a form of blended learning, some technological, theoretical, and methodological considerations of the blended learning sections presented next may be subsumed into the more concise sections to follow on flipped classrooms.

Method

The university had formerly administered TOEFL tests to all first-year students, as of several years ago. However, no significant difference was found between pretests upon entry and posttests. For instance, the average TOEFL score among 500 economics majors was 430 in April of 2011 and then 427 in January of 2012. Core first-year English classes consisted of Fundamental English, taught by native English teachers; Writing and Communication, taught by Japanese English teachers, and Reading, taught by Japanese English teachers. These two English courses taught by Japanese English teachers were taught mainly in Japanese. Spurred by the disappointing results of the TOEFL posttest average scores, the blended and flipped learning program was introduced in 2013, in order to improve English proficiency among economics majors. Obari has carried out several empirical case studies since 2013, some of which are introduced in this section as follows:

The blended learning study was conducted over a period of 9 months during two academic semesters (April 2013 to December 2013). A total of 90 undergraduates, all native speakers of Japanese studying at a private university in Tokyo, were the participants of the study. The students were administered TOEIC as a pretest in April 2013 and again as a posttest in December 2013, the purpose of which was to ascertain the effectiveness of the blended learning (BL) program.

The research questions targeted in this study were as follows:

Are blended learning (BL) activities using mobile devices useful in improving students' overall English skills?
Can online TED Talks and the ATR CALL BRIX program help to improve the TOEIC scores of native Japanese students of EFL?
Can Globalvoice CALL helps to improve the English pronunciation of Japanese EFL students in terms of words and prosody?
Can the online Newton m-Learning program helps to improve the TOEIC scores of native Japanese students of EFL?

The blended learning activities included the following: (1) students watching online TED talks with the use of PC or mobile devices, (2) students spending extensive time watching TED Talks during their commuting hours and writing a 300-word summary of each lecture each week, (3) students presenting oral summaries of the TED talks to their classmates both face-to-face and in front of the class, (4) students using Globalvoice CALL software for TED talk summaries to brush up on their English pronunciation and prosody before presentations, (5) students using the online Newton m-Learning program by PC or mobile devices during their free time, and (6) students using the online ATR CALL BRIX program to improve their English proficiency and TOEIC scores in the classroom and during their free time with the use of PCs and mobile devices.

At the end of the course, a questionnaire was administered to students after their exposure to the above activities for the purpose of ascertaining their impressions of the BL activities.

To introduce the technologies utilized, TED Talks are widely considered useful online learning resources for multidisciplinary content of contemporary relevance, and are conducive to m-Learning, whereby learning can take place at any time and any place, provided robust mobile technologies are available to learners. Newton m-Learning, the ATR CALL BRIX program, and Globalvoice CALL are among the other useful online learning resources available that the following aims to show are consistent with the above theoretical considerations and thus conducive to m-Learning.

TED Talks

TED is a foundation that, for the purposes of this book, makes professional quality presentations in many fields available freely from its Web site http://www.ted.com or through various platforms including YouTube, podcasts, television, radio, and, significantly for the purposes of this chapter, mobile apps for smartphones, tablets, and other devices that can play digital videos. TED talks utilized for educational purposes typically feature innovative research presented concisely in less than 18 min, and made as interesting as possible with various media and appeals to human interest. Thus, TED talks can serve as a relatively painless way for learners to explore a wide range of fields. For nonnative English users at intermediate or advanced levels in listening comprehension, the recorded videos available online allow to control the experience such as repeated viewing and access to talks on the go with mobile apps.

Globalvoice CALL Software

How can Japanese EFL learners learn to speak more intelligible English for international communication? There exist many factors in evaluating nonnative speakers of English. Rhythmic accent and pauses are considered more important than segmental features in English utterances to make speech intelligible. In this regard, prosodic features such as intonation and the rhythm of the language are crucial to comprehensible speech.

One of the main goals of English education in Japan is to help Japanese speak English intelligibly, so they can be more clearly understood while taking part in international communication. Several parameters such as speech duration, speech power, F0 (pitch), and the ratio of vowel and consonant length are all introduced to determine how much Japanese students can improve their English pronunciation and overall proficiency by using Globalvoice CALL (Obari 2013) software (pictured in Figs. 5.1 and 5.2).

Globalvoice CALL is software into which students input any words or sentences to practice their pronunciation via specialized speech training. This software can enable Japanese students to correct their pronunciation by helping them improve their prosodic and segmental features. About 84 % of 150 Japanese EFL students who used this software reported that it would be very useful for practicing English pronunciation and prosody.

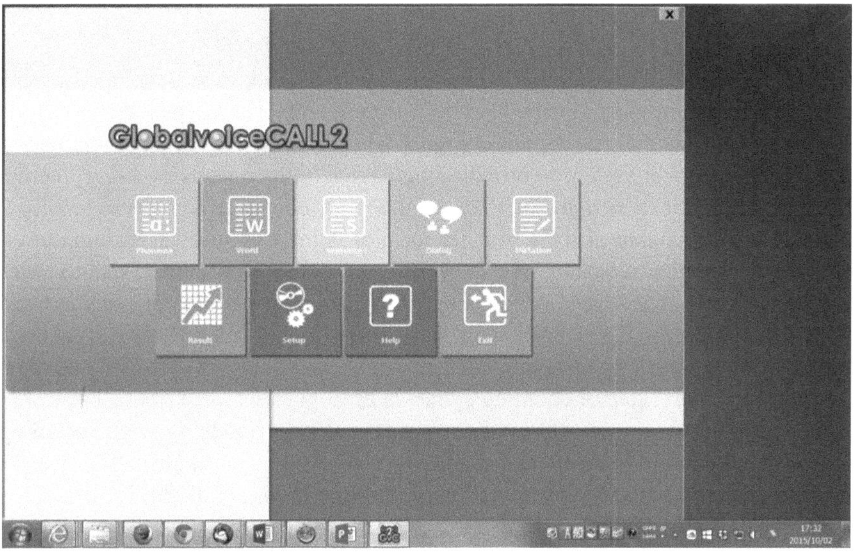

Fig. 5.1 Display of the Globalvoice CALL software

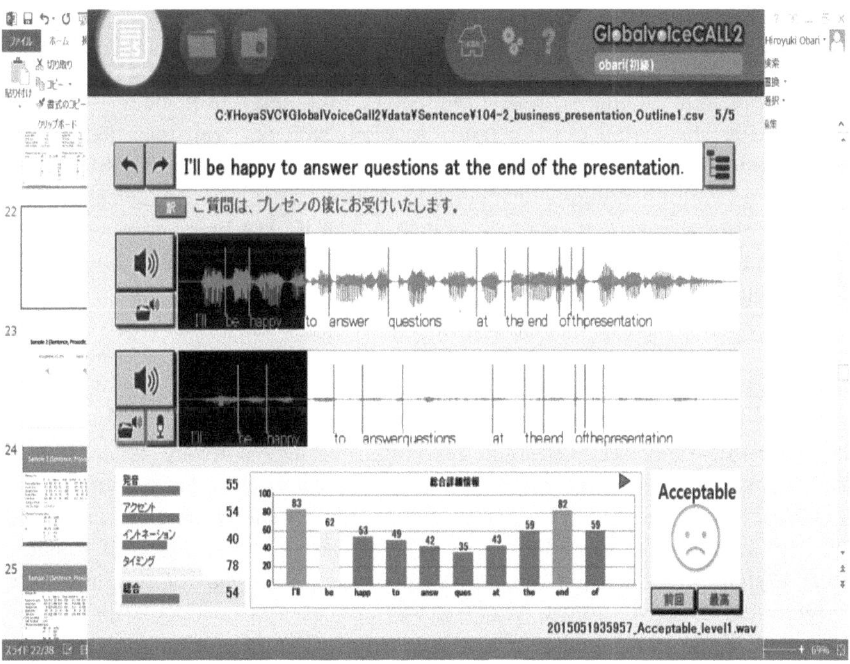

Fig. 5.2 Display of English phonemes

ATR CALL BRIX Program

ATR CALL BRIX is an English e-Learning system which was developed by the Advanced Telecommunication Research Institution (ATR) and expanded by Uchida Yoko Co., Ltd. mainly into Japanese higher education institutions and companies. This is a client server system to provide English learning contents by using Internet Explorer®. Most of its system administrators allow students or employees to access the server from outside of their Intranet to offer them a ubiquitous learning environment. Through a sequence of experiments by ATR, a bottom-up method was developed as an efficient way to learn English for Japanese people. This method was adopted for the ATR CALL BRIX for basic English skill training. For instance, a learner starts training by listening to a minimal pair contrast exercise, and then moves onto the next step of counting syllables of English words. For this basic skill training, a database of 15,000 English words had been made as well, including sample speech from over 30 native speakers of American English. Every item contains distractors for efficient vocabulary building (Obari et al. 2013a, b).

The ATR CALL BRIX also offers the TOEIC® Test Official Training Course which includes the official TOEIC contents offered by ETS, a nonprofit organization which develops and provides various academic assessments. In Japan, TOEIC® has in recent years become the most common assessment test to measure business English communication skills. According to public data of The Institute for International Business Communication (IIBC) which provides the TOEIC test in Japan, 2,312,000 people took the test in 2012. This course is designed not only for practice tests to get higher scores on the real TOEIC® tests. It includes vocabulary development, shadowing practice, and dictation exercises with qualified TOEIC official contents in order to build up and improve English skills. ATR CALL BRIX is thus an e-Learning system which helps learners enhance their English skills with its course for basic skill training as well as a TOEIC test preparation course for accessing a server from smartphones and tablet devices to provide learners with a more ubiquitous learning environment (Obari et al. 2013a, b).

Newton m-Learning Program

Newton m-Learning TLT (testing, learning, training) software is a form of Web-Based Training (WBT) developed for e-Learning in academic settings. Individual learners are able to ubiquitously review their studies anytime, anywhere. Teachers are also able to uniformly manage the progress and results of students' research studies. As a result, this software can be employed for assignments in everyday classes apart from CALL and PC labs, as it is conducive for learning regardless of the time or place when used with tablet PCs or smartphones, and claims the potential for improvements over traditional study modalities. The convenience of the software stems from the fact that the educational TLT software materials are an Internet-based form of m-Learning, and are predominantly drill based, problem exercise materials (Obari et al. 2013a, b).

First, the program extracts the necessary contents on the basis of each student's records in order to present them with their targeted assignments. Then, the students' tests, learning, and teaching are all repeated automatically, and their records are accumulated in reiterations of the learning cycle until they become proficient. The overall systems are called "TLT Software" and are the only computerized educational materials to have acquired patents in Japan and US (domestic patent No. 3820421, US patent No. 5888071). The following three functionalities form the backbone of these patents:

(1) Staged learning functionality: control of learning in three steps: Testing, Learning, and Training (forming the initials for TLT).
(2) Automatic learning functionality: automatically executes weak point extraction/repeat learning.
(3) Automatic decision functionality: automatically determines true/false answers with the first sound character for an answer (one-touch input).

Furthermore, the systems control problem arrangement, question order, and step progression in the materials on the basis of these functions it has been patented in both the US and Japan.

Newton e-Learning materials for the TOEIC test enable studying commensurate with every proficiency stage possible, from beginner to mastery. Moreover, it contains a total of over 24,000 learning challenges. Overall, they are composed of two courses (A and B), each with the aim of improving TOEIC Bridge and TOEIC test scores. Also, both A and B courses are comprised of two Exercise Materials and Test Material types: A. The Exercise Materials include four sections: Problems, Basics, Dictation, and Vocabulary Training types, with exercises being presented in separate parts, B. The Test Materials provide fixed Web Test A/B tests (8 total times), and short Web Test A/B by Part tests (20 total times).

Use of the teaching materials management functions allows one to view the progress of students both individually and as a group, to have a grasp of their learning status, to make changes to various settings, and to download data. Moreover, interactive functionality can be exploited as well. Since 2012, Newton e-Learning has been supporting not only Windows XP, Vista, 7 and 8 (Internet Explorer 7 or above), but also Macintosh (Mac OS X 10.4–10.8 with Safari 4, 5 and 6), the iPad (Mobile Safari), and smartphones for wider learning settings (Obari et al. 2013a, b).

Assessment of the Blended Learning Activities

To assess the results, a sampling of the data is summarized and interpreted in the following sections, including the results from TOEIC tests, which revealed that the students' overall English proficiency had improved after their exposure to the BL activities. Also included are some of the results of the survey administered to students for the purpose of attaining feedback on how they felt about using the BL activities to practice their English language skills.

TOEIC Test Results

The TOEIC results revealed that the mean scores significantly increased from 570 (SD = 102) in the pretest to 687 (SD = 108) in the posttest for the 3rd year students, and increased from 382 (SD = 102) to 573 (SD = 120) for the 1st year students. The TOEIC pre and posttest results were analyzed using a t-test, indicating that the difference between pre and posttest scores of both student classes were statistically significant at a 1 % level. The improvement in scores would seem to indicate that the utilization of a learning environment integrating a BL environment with m-Learning helped the students to improve their overall English proficiency.

Questionnaire

A survey was administered to the participants after being exposed to the blended-learning program incorporating TED Talks and the use of emerging technologies. In response to the survey question, "Did you find the TED Talks useful in improving your English proficiency?," 91 % of 90 students felt that the online lectures were very useful. In response to similar survey questions about the ATR CALL BRIX program and Newton m-Learning program, 89 and 76 %, respectively, felt that they were very effective and useful. And in response to the question, "To what extent did you use mobile technologies to learn online TED talks and Newton m-Learning program?," 30 % of students responded that they had used their mobile devices in those ways to study English online.

Assessment of English Writing, Oral Summaries, and English Pronunciation

At the start of the semester, the students made numerous grammatical and structural mistakes in their summary writings of TED Talks. However, by the end of term their English writings for the most part had fewer grammatical errors, were better organized, and were longer in duration. In addition, by comparing the first and final oral summaries, many of the students demonstrated significant improvements in their oral skills, particularly in terms of segmental and prosodic features, including pitch, intonation, accent, timing, and vowel duration because of the use of Globalvoice CALL software.

Flipped Classroom Project 1

As a reversal to traditional learning, the flipped classroom is a new educational environment which is quickly gaining in popularity among educators around the world. In a flipped classroom, students learn the course lectures and content from online videos, materials, and other learning tools before coming to class, and spend a bulk of their classroom time asking questions and being engaged in interactive discussions.

The study was carried out from April 2014 to January 2015 at Aoyama Gakuin University in Tokyo, Japan, and targeted 60 first-year undergraduate students to evaluate the effectiveness of a flipped classroom compared to a traditional classroom learning environment. The experimental group was exposed to flipped lessons for 24 weeks using the Oxford University Press hybrid e-book English textbook *Lecture Ready 1* (Sarosy and Sherak 2013a). The students were required to watch the course video lectures and online English learning materials using mobile technologies before coming to each class, and then created PPT slides for classroom presentations and discussions. The students shared their presentations and interacted with each other during the regular classes. A control group of students was taught using traditional methods with the paper textbook *Lecture Ready 1*, but with no flipped lesson contents. The control students also watched the video lectures and answered the textbook questions, but only during regular classroom periods, including discussions among themselves during the 24-week period.

An assessment of pretreatment and posttreatment TOEIC scores showed that the students exposed to the flipped lessons improved from 474 (SD 111) to 649 (SD 96), which was greater than that of the control group students, who improved from 484 (SD 123) to 617 (SD 115). By the end of the eight-month training period, the experimental group students had completed 80 % of the course contents and substantially improved their overall reading, listening, and oral communication skills through the online English lectures with flipped lessons.

Flipped Classroom Project 2

The second study was conducted over a 10 month period during two academic semesters (April 2014 to January 2015). A total of 25 undergraduates were the participants of the study. All of the participants were native speakers of Japanese studying at a private university in Tokyo. The students were administered TOEIC as a pretest in April 2014 and again as a posttest in January 2015. The purpose of this was to serve as a measurement to help determine if the students' scores would improve as a result their exposure to the BL and flipped classroom activities, and thereby help ascertain the effectiveness of the lessons. The research questions of this study were as follows:

(1) Are blended learning (BL) activities using mobile devices beneficial in improving Japanese EFL students' English proficiency?

(2) Are flipped classroom activities using Lecture Ready 2 and the ATR CALL Brix program with a tablet or smartphone useful for improving the TOEIC scores of Japanese EFL students?
(3) Can Globalvoice CALL helps to improve the English pronunciation skills of Japanese EFL students in terms of prosodic and segmental features?

The blended and flipped learning activities of this study included the following: (1) students watched the online digital textbook *Lecture Ready 2* (Sarosy and Sherak 2013b). using a PC and with their mobile devices; (2) students spent extensive time watching the lectures with the support of COOORI (Web-based language learning software downloadable from iTunes) during their commuting hours and later wrote a 300-word summary of one lecture per week; (3) students created PowerPoint presentations and presented oral summaries of the e-textbook lectures to their classmates both face-to-face and in front of the entire class; (4) students used Globalvoice CALL software along with their *Lecture Ready 2* summaries to attempt to improve their English pronunciation in terms of segmental and prosodic features before their presentations; (5) students used the online program Newton m-Learning with the use of a PC and mobile device during their free time; and (6) students used the online program ATR CALL Brix to improve their TOEIC scores and overall English proficiency in and out of the classroom during their free time with the use of a PC and mobile device. At the end of the course, a questionnaire was administered to the students after their exposure to the above training activities.

It can be seen from the above list of activities, when compared with the previous study of blended learning (BL) that the flipped classroom represents an attempt at the fullest realization of the potential of BL.

Assessment of the Blended and Flipped Learning Activities

A sampling of the data results is presented below, including the results from TOEIC tests, which revealed that the students' overall English proficiency had improved after their exposure to the blended and flipped learning activities. Also included are some of the results of the survey administered to students for the purpose of attaining feedback on how they felt about all the activities. Twenty-five students took the OPIc computer speaking test a total of twice (in April 2014 and again in January 2015) to measure their oral proficiency.

TOEIC Test Results

The TOEIC results revealed that the mean scores increased from a mean TOEIC score of 577 (SD: 132) to a mean score of 758 (SD: 105), which would seem to indicate that the students improved their overall English proficiency. TOEIC pre and posttest results were analyzed using a t-test, indicating that the difference between pre and posttest scores of both classes were statistically significant at a 1 % level.

OPIc Computer Speaking Test

An increase of roughly 24 % in the OPIc speaking test was observed between the pretest and posttest. This improvement would seem to indicate that the utilization of a learning environment of blended and flipped lessons did help the students to improve their overall English proficiency (cf. Fig. 5.3 below).

Questionnaire

A survey was administered to the participants after their exposure to the blended learning lessons incorporating *Lecture Ready 2* and TED Talks through the use of mobile technologies. In response to the survey question, "did you find the digital *Lecture Ready 2* (1) useful in improving your English proficiency?," 91 % of students felt that the online lectures were very useful. In response to the questions "did you find the ATR CALL Brix program (2), Newton m-Learning program (3), and Globalvoice CALL software (4) useful in improving your English proficiency and pronunciation?," the percentage of students responded that they felt they were effective and useful were, respectively, as follows: (2) 82 %, (3) 84 %, and (4) 91 %. Finally, in response to the question "to what extent did you use mobile technologies to study with the online Newton m-Learning program?," 30 % responded that they had used their mobile devices to study the online English programs.

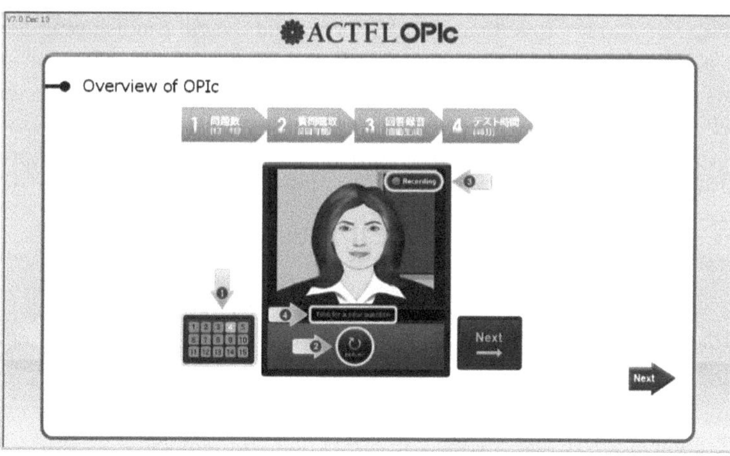

Fig. 5.3 OPIc computerized speaking proficiency test screen shot

Flipped Classroom Project 3

The third study was conducted over a ten-month period during two academic semesters (April 2015 to January 2016). A total of 24 undergraduates were the participants of the study. All of the participants were native speakers of Japanese studying at a private university in Tokyo. The students were administered TOEIC as a pretest in April 2015 and again as a posttest in January 2016. The purpose of this was to serve as a measurement to help determine if the students' scores would improve as a result their exposure to the BL and flipped classroom activities, and thereby help ascertain the effectiveness of the lessons. The research questions of this study were as follows:

(1) Are blended learning (BL) activities using mobile devices beneficial in improving Japanese EFL students' English proficiency?
(2) Are flipped classroom activities using *Lecture Ready 3*, Newton e-Learning TOEIC Practice Kit, and the ATR CALL Brix program with a tablet or smartphone useful for improving the TOEIC scores of Japanese EFL students?
(3) Is blended learning (BL) useful in changing students' worldviews?

The blended and flipped learning activities of this study included the following: (1) students listened to the online digital textbook *Lecture Ready 3* (Sarosy and Sherak 2013c), using a PC and with their mobile devices; (2) students spent extensive time watching the e-textbook lectures with the support of COOORI (Web-based language learning software downloadable from iTunes) during their commuting hours and later wrote a 300-word summary of one lecture per week; (3) students created PowerPoint presentations and presented oral summaries of the e-textbook lectures to their classmates both face to face and in front of the entire class; (4) students read several articles related to worldviews and made PPT presentations; (5) students used the online program Newton m-Learning with a PC and mobile device during their free time; and (6) students used the online program ATR CALL Brix to improve their TOEIC scores and overall English proficiency in and out of the classroom during their free time with the use of a PC and mobile device. At the end of the course, a questionnaire was administered to the students after their exposure to the above training activities.

It can be seen from the above list of activities, when compared with the previous study of blended learning (BL) that the flipped classroom represents an attempt at the fullest realization of the potential of BL.

Assessment of the Blended and Flipped Learning Activities

A sampling of the data results is presented below, including the results from CASEC computerized tests, which revealed that the students' overall English proficiency had improved after their exposure to the blended and flipped learning activities. Also included are some of the results of the survey administered to students for the purpose of attaining feedback on how they felt about all the activities. Twenty-four students took the OPIc computer speaking test a total of twice (in May 2015 and again in January 2016) to measure their oral proficiency.

CASEC Test Results

The computer-based CASEC Test (cf. http://casec.evidus.com) results revealed that the mean scores increased from a mean score of 626 (SD: 88) to a mean score of 721 (SD: 63), which would seem to indicate that the students improved their overall English proficiency. CASEC pre and posttest results were analyzed using a t-test, indicating that the difference between pre and posttest scores of both classes were statistically significant at a 1 % level.

OPIc Computer Speaking Test

An increase of roughly 20 % in the OPIc speaking test was observed between the pretest and posttest. This improvement would seem to indicate that the utilization of a learning environment of blended and flipped lessons did help the students to improve their overall English proficiency.

Questionnaire

A survey was administered to the participants after their exposure to the blended learning lessons incorporating worldview studies through the use of mobile technologies. In this case study, students were asked to respond to worldview-related questions. Did their world views change after they joined this course? From their essay writings, based upon the pre- and post-questionnaire, most of the responses indicated that their worldviews were more open-minded, starting to see invisible parts of another culture and understanding the concept of worldview presented in several articles from two Oxford scholars concerning ontological and epistemological scientific worldviews. "Language as a worldview" was held to be a very important concept in language learning while students endeavored to improve their English proficiency. Through this seminar, the 24 students improved their English proficiency and expanded their worldviews to be more internationally minded.

Limitations of the Studies

Possible limitations of the blended and flipped learning studies were as follows:

(1) Although students were encouraged to use mobile devices to do the learning activities, for some activities they felt it would be more convenient to use PCs instead of mobile devices. COOORI and Newton e-Learning TOEIC Practice Kit were easily accessed with mobile devices. 100 % mobile use actually was confirmed when tracking how much students logged into study, although the detailed data are not shown in this chapter.
(2) *Lecture Ready 2* (Sarosy and Sherak 2013b) and *Lecture Ready 3* (Sarosy and Sherak 2013c) were available mainly as e-books for iPad. Thus, in most cases students both accessed these materials and prepared their presentations by iPad (see Fig. 5.4 below) to present and discuss among the participants. However, in some cases, they might have used PCs to study some materials. How they learned and what they learned could not be exactly observed while they were actively involved in classroom discussions and presentations.
(3) Precisely what materials students were using with mobile devices or PCs, or their combination, was not completely tracked. Thus, it might be difficult to assert that mobile learning helped students make more progress than would otherwise be the case in improving their English proficiency. It would rather be safer to say that the integration of mobile devices with PCs could enhance learning in flipped and blended environments.
(4) In the case of classroom activities, all the lessons were recorded with camcorders to be preserved on hard disks for three years to further investigate how students were engaged in active learning (cf. Fig. 5.4 below), while, of course, out-of-classroom activities were not observed.

Fig. 5.4 Flipped learning activity: student made presentation by iPad

Conclusion

Mobile m-Learning can be motivating to learners to help improve their foreign language skills, as it offers them a rich, informal, contextual, and ubiquitous learning environment. This case study focused on examining a variety of emerging technologies, from speech recognition to Web-based learning, to help determine the effectiveness of blended learning and flipped classroom activities. Various emerging technologies such as ATR CALL BRIX, a mobile learning-oriented TOEIC Practice program, Course Power, online TED Talks, and other learning materials were utilized, including an empirical study that indicated their effect on improving the TOEIC scores of native Japanese speaking undergraduates.

The first phase of the study targeted approximately 90 Japanese undergraduates who spent approximately 50 total hours to complete an online TOEIC course with flipped classroom learning materials using a PC and mobile technologies for the purpose of enhancing their English proficiency. By the end of the second term, students had completed nearly 100 % of the online course contents and written 90 TED Talk summaries. The students were administered TOEIC as a pretest in April 2013 and as a posttest in December 2013. The results indicated that their mean TOEIC score had improved from 570 (SD 102) to 687 (SD 108) for third-year students during the nine-month period while being exposed to the blended learning environments. After the students were engaged in the flipped classroom lessons with online materials, and had delivered their English presentations while engaging in Digital Storytelling and writing blogs, they exhibited a high level of English writing performance, particularly during the second semester, in terms of their summary writings of the TED Talks. A questionnaire was also administered to the students, which indicated that the students were satisfied by their exposure to the blended learning activities.

An assessment of pre and posttraining TOEIC scores revealed that TED Talks activities, the ATR CALL BRIX program, the Newton m-Learning program, and the use of emerging technologies had a positive effect on the students' overall English skills. In addition, the students' listening and oral communication skills improved as a result of integrating the targeted e-Learning and m-Learning activities. A questionnaire administered after their exposure to the BL activities indicated that the students were satisfied with the variety of online courses mentioned above and motivated by the BL environment incorporating m-Learning. The students' English writing and oral summary skills also improved after their exposure to the online TED talks and the use of Globalvoice CALL software.

With regard to the Flipped Classroom Project 1 and 2, an assessment of pre and posttraining TOEIC and OPIc scores (Project 2) revealed that various types of online materials and activities included in our study had a positive effect on the students' overall English skills. Additionally, the students' listening and oral communication skills improved as a result of integrating blended and flipped learning activities through m-Learning. The questionnaire indicated that they were satisfied with the variety of online course materials and programs and were motivated by the BL environment incorporating m-Learning. The students' English writing and oral summary skills also improved after their exposure to *Lecture Ready 2* and Globalvoice CALL software.

Overall, these results would seem to indicate that the blended learning using mobile technologies can be effectively integrated into the language learning curriculum and can play a positive role in improving students' language proficiency. Additionally, instructor observations of the BL activities revealed that the students were excited by using a variety of emerging new technologies, which enabled them to effectively learn English by accessing a variety of learning materials from their mobile devices. M-Learning helped to increase the amount of comprehensible English input with the aid of recently developed learning technologies. It was also highly motivating to students by offering them a rich, informal, contextual, and ubiquitous learning environment which enabled them to control their learning opportunities or occasions (time), environment (space), and speed (pace).

Recommendations for Other Institutions

There are now many online e-Learning materials available to teach EFL, so institutions need to choose among them judiciously. The technologies utilized in this study were each found to be effective for e-Learning in a blended or flipped classroom approach. The Newton e-Learning Practice Kit is recommended to improve the TOEIC scores of EFL learners. Students could study those materials entirely using mobile technologies as well. Another software solution recommended is COOORI, which can be directly linked to whichever textbook is used, in order to study vocabulary with the support of artificial intelligence.

In addition, Globalvoice CALL software was found to be well-suited to teaching segmental and prosodic features of English, especially as it allows any words or sentences students make to be processed by the software, so students can practice English pronunciation and prosody. Some software solutions become part of the campus infrastructure and support various classes, which would be more efficient than each teacher ordering software without curriculum integration.

Then there was the example in this and the previous chapter of publisher materials that can be used as paper textbooks or e-books, with audio and video available at a dedicated Web site for purchasers (Sarosy and Sherak 2013a, b). The off-the-shelf approach could be recommended for convenience, especially for universities with limited experience in developing their own materials or finding suitable open educational resources. Speaking of the latter, Aoyama Gakuin University was shown in this chapter to have combined purchased software and e-textbooks with freely available online resources, chiefly TED talks, furthermore leveraging the mobile phones nearly all students carry to aim for ubiquitous m-Learning. The more multifaceted the approach, covering all available devices and media, and the more tightly and seamlessly integrated into the campus-wide infrastructure and curriculum, the more effective the results could be for student learning outcomes.

References

Bandura, A. (1977). *Social learning theory*. New York: General Learning Press.

Burr, V. (1995). *An introduction to social constructionism*. London: Routledge.

Burr, V. (2003). *Social constructionism* (2nd ed.). London: Routledge.

Chinnery, G. (2006). Going to the MALL: Mobile assisted-learning. *Language Learning and Technology, 10*(1), 9–16.

Dörnyei, Z. (2009). *The psychology of second language acquisition*. Oxford, UK: Oxford University Press.

Dörnyei, Z. (2010). Researching motivation: From integrativeness to the ideal L2 self. In S. Hunston & D. Oake (Eds.), *Introducing applied linguistics: Concepts and skills* (pp. 74–83). London: Routledge.

Fujimoto, C. (2013). Perceptions of mobile learning in Australia: How ready are learners to study on the move? *JALT CALL Journal, 8*(3), 165–195.

Gardner, R. (2007). Motivation and second language acquisition. *Porta Linguarum, 8*, 9–20.

Gualtieri, M. (2011, April). Mobile app design best practices: When it comes to designing the mobile user experience (UX), context is king. Retrieved from http://www.forrester.com/rb/Research/mobile_app_design_best_practices/q/id/59132/t/2

Kukulska-Hulme, A., & Shield, L. (2008). An overview of mobile assisted language learning: Can mobile devices support collaborative practice in speaking and listening? *ReCALL, 20*, 271–289. Retrieved from http://vsportal2007.googlepages.com/Kukulska_Hulme_and_Shield_2007.pdf

Levy, M. (1997). *Computer-assisted language learning: Context and conceptualization*. Oxford, UK: Oxford University Press.

Miangah, T. M., & Nezarat, A. (2012). Mobile-assisted language learning. *International Journal of Distributed and Parallel Systems, 3*, 310–319. Retrieved from http://airccse.org/journal/ijdps/papers/0112ijdps26.pdf

Obari, H. (2013). Globalvoice CALL. Retrieved from http://voicetext.jp/gv/pro_gvc_case008.html

Obari, H., Kojima, H., & Itahashi, S. (2010). Empowering EFL learners to interact effectively in a blended learning environment. In J. Herrington & B. Hunter (Eds.), *Proceedings of the World Conference on Educational Multimedia, Hypermedia and Telecommunications 2010* (pp. 3438–3447). Chesapeake, VA: AACE.

Obari, H., Nagae, T., Yamagishi, N., & Tanaka, Y. (2013a, July 11). The effect of using on-line TOEIC related materials using mobile technologies. In *World CALL 2013*, Courseware showcase, p. 198.

Obari, H., Suto, A. Kobayashi, Y., Ogihara, T., & Lambacher, S. (2013b, July 12). The effects of CALL software in teaching English pronunciation and TOEIC. In *World CALL 2013*, Courseware showcase, p. 197.

Ryan, R., & Deci, E. (2000). Intrinsic and extrinsic motivations: Classic definitions and new directions. *Contemporary Educational Psychology, 25*, 54–67.

Sarosy, P. & Sherak, K. (2013a). *Lecture ready 1: Strategies for academic listening and speaking*. Oxford: Oxford University Press (textbook, Website & e-book).

Sarosy, P. & Sherak, K. (2013b). *Lecture ready 2: Strategies for academic listening and speaking*. Oxford: Oxford University Press (textbook, Website & e-book).

Sarosy, P. & Sherak, K. (2013c). *Lecture ready 3: Strategies for academic listening and speaking*. Oxford: Oxford University Press (textbook, Website & e-book).

Sherimon, P. C., Vinu, P. V., & Reshmy, K. (2011). Enhancing the learning experience in blended learning systems: A semantic approach. In *Proceedings of the 2011 conference on communication, computing & security* (pp. 449–452). ACM.

Singh, H., & Reed, C. (2001). A white paper: Achieving success with blended learning. *Centra Software, 1*.

Stockwell, G. (2008). Investigating learner preparedness for and usage patterns of mobile learning. *ReCALL, 20*(3), 253–270.

Stockwell, G. (Ed.). (2012a). *Computer-assisted language learning: Diversity in research and practice*. Cambridge, UK: Cambridge University Press.

Stockwell, G. (2012b). Mobile-assisted language learning. In M. Thomas, H. Reiders, & M. Warshauer (Eds.), *Contemporary computer-assisted language learning*. London: Bloomsbury Publishing.

Thornton, P., & Houser, C. (2005). Using mobile phones in English education in Japan. *Journal of Computer Assisted Learning*, *21*(3), 217–228.

Vinu, P. V., Sherimon, P. C., & Krishnan, R. (2011). Towards pervasive mobile learning–The vision of 21st century. *Procedia—Social and Behavioural Sciences, 15*, 3067–3073. doi:10.1016/j.sbspro.2011.04.247

Wilson, D., & Smilanich, E. (2005). *The other blended learning*. San Francisco, CA: Pfeiffer Publishing.

Chapter 6
Conclusion: Implementing Language Learning in a Mobile-Oriented Society

Abstract This concluding chapter summarizes the main points of the previous five chapters, with conclusions and further recommendations for other institutions. It reiterates the methodology introduced in Chap. 1 to define mobile language learning, then briefly summarizes its history in Japan. Some recurring issues led to conclusions such as that small screen sizes could be tolerated because of Japan's long tenure as a mobile-oriented society. The sociocultural approach in Chap. 2 represented a global consensus among humanistic educators that inspired the pedagogy behind the case studies in Chaps. 3, 4 and 5. Mobile learning was found to bring out aspects of sociocultural theory through factors such as user autonomy. Its effectiveness for EFL should encourage readers to implement m-learning in their own contexts.

Summation, Recommendations, and Conclusions

This book began with an original approach to define concepts in academic fields by contextualizing technical terms into their cultural, disciplinary, and temporal dimensions. As one result of this analysis, mobile language learning is preferred to MALL because the focus of the former is less on the technology and more on the mobility of the learner. MALL nevertheless occupies a place in disciplinary usage after CAI and CALL, historically, but prior to ubiquitous language learning, which is a future prediction of seamless unobstructed learning at everyone's fingertips, which in turn can suggest principles, criteria, and goals to aim for next with the technology and pedagogical understanding available today.

Chapter 1 then traced the historical development of MALL in Japan from the mobile Internet in the late 1990s to recent years when popularization of m-Learning led to a profusion of experimental studies. Now that some of the earliest initiatives from around 2000 have been presented, future research in other regions can draw from this hitherto unpublished history, for example, to compare other cultures with Japan in terms of receptivity toward certain technologies, or ostensibly universal factors such as screen size. Japan was shown to be a mobile-oriented society from

S. McCarty et al., *Implementing Mobile Language Learning Technologies in Japan*, SpringerBriefs in Education, DOI 10.1007/978-981-10-2451-1_6

the earliest stage, challenging language teachers, particularly those who rely on paper media or even computers, to harness technologies students already use, and the networking skills they already display, for more effective language learning and authentic L2 use in mobile communication and online communities.

The case studies in this book opted to present a diverse range of institutions and pedagogical experiments with the technological affordances available since the advent of the Internet, rather than bulking up quantitatively in one type of practice and missing the whole picture of this era. At the same time, Chap. 2 on mobile language learning pedagogy focuses on a sociocultural approach that pioneering researchers have found most effective for humanistic m-Learning. While Chap. 1 focuses on Japan, Chap. 2 thus focuses on the leading pedagogy characterizing this era of rapidly advancing technologies applicable to learning that is both more autonomous and more social than ever. At the disciplinary level, the sociocultural perspective is most prominent in the literature on m-Learning pedagogy; while on the cultural level, this approach is both widely accepted and informed by practice in diverse human contexts in the world.

Each of the case studies followed a similar outline, explaining the institutional context, rationale, and theoretical framework for the m-Learning practices, then presenting and discussing the results, with recommendations for other institutions. A monograph of this type differs from a journal or a collection of papers, as a book provides the space to tell a story. Thus, the authors attempted to describe each situation and practice fully enough to inform the decision-making process of practitioners at other institutions and in other countries.

The first case study sharpens the sociocultural focus on teaching EFL in Asia and closely applies the approach in a culture with similar predispositions. For in Japan, human relations are valued above all, with mobile phones as an extension of each individual, keeping them not only well informed to navigate daily life but also well connected to their peer group and to significant others. Chapter 3 describes and reports on two small-scale experiments in mobile phone group chats with the app LINE, already widely used by students for personal communications. While no conclusive claims are made, the details provide an example that other teachers and researchers may consider in their own situation. The fact that the students agreed to use their mobile phones for extracurricular exposure to English outside of their major fields and did not drop out of the experiment may have pragmatic implications beyond the inconclusive improvements in English proficiency. One perennial question in the literature was whether or not students would willingly let teachers harness their personal communication devices for educational purposes. The findings of the authors in Chap. 3 and when touching upon past experiments with social media in Chap. 4 support the hypothesis that students *are* willing to communicate authentically in their L2, to cross the teacher–student social divide, and to show investment in learning by using their personally vital mobile devices, *provided* the approach sufficiently respects the cultural contours of the students.

The quantitative results of Chap. 3 showed modest gains in English proficiency using standard measures, more so when students composed their own English than when using an automatic translation app, which would be controversial if resorted to in place of student effort or attention. At the very least, the mobile phone group chats placed English in front of the students for possible response or analysis where communication would have otherwise been conducted wholly in Japanese.

There was also questionnaire feedback bringing student perspectives into clearer view. The experiment was well received in terms of the primary informant data, taxing neither for the students nor for the teacher who provided only orientation to the activity without explicit language teaching. This model could be replicated or developed in other settings with any kind of mobile devices all students are using.

Further research could investigate the causality involved in the positive correlation found between writing more and improved reading, particularly in a mobile online community of practice. Factors to investigate include any thresholds or levels of L2 proficiency necessary to participate, the interaction itself in a foreign language regardless of the media, the social context, the sense of community established, the efficacy of a community of practice as theorized, along with the affordances of the software such as LINE in this case. The mobility of learners with smartphones or other Internet-connected portable or wearable devices should be compared with the offline or face-to-face limitations of institutional education hitherto taken for granted, as online communication anywhere and anytime manifestly affords more opportunities for interaction in any language than would otherwise be possible.

Chapter 4 showed that when a university is committed to women's empowerment, the myth of women being weak in technology use is demonstrably shattered. It was a female Japanese professor and alumnus of the 2-year college who initiated having an iPod for all students, stocked with faculty-made English listening files, when the 4-year university started in 2004, first in the world. This chapter showed technologies integrated into the curriculum campus-wide, rather than experiments by an individual or division. The change to giving all incoming students an iPad in 2012 was also a pioneer initiative, with faculty-made e-books, campus-wide wi-fi, and a readiness for pedagogical applications of Internet access. Legal and other obstacles to m-Learning or blended learning between classes, such as the personal information privacy law, were overcome by making mobile devices an extension of the campus infrastructure.

The chapter explained podcasting, which made the iPod an accessory to online communication or 'spoken Internet to go.' Student-generated content was shown to enhance integrative motivation as students did not just imagine the community of English users through the Web but joined it and found an appreciative audience. The iPod represented an intermediate stage in both Internet access and usability, as wireless-ready mobile communication and software processing of multimedia files became easier, faster, and more seamless with the advent of smartphones and tablet computers like iPad.

The chapter further detailed iPad functions available and readily utilizable for study, including homework, across the curriculum where all students major in English. Also introduced were the e-books used as textbooks in all core first year classes integrating the four skills, downloaded by each student to their iPad from the campus server, or from the publisher in the case of some second year listening classes. Moreover, the Apple iBook program and many of its functions to create not just electronic texts but interactive exercises were introduced. Readers who are considering going beyond off-the-shelf electronic materials for content-based or specialized courses might find the experience of this university of reference.

Having the faculty integrated along with the curriculum, working together on e-books and mutual concerns, and providing IT classes in the vernacular, hands-on training for students, staff, and part-time as well as full-time teachers, all accrue to the effectiveness of technological and pedagogical integration.

Various assessments were cited, in the form of annual questionnaires and focus groups, which showed how students preferred to utilize mobile devices, including their own smartphone in many cases, which helped refine further practices and more focused assessments. Japanese students in such an encouraging environment can become quite individualistic and outspoken, resulting in a variety of feedback. Through iterations of assessments, some limitations of tablets, and e-books were frankly identified by students. Most may be solved in the future as software and usability improve, but the perennial limitations of screen size appear as noted in previous studies cited in this book. While are individual differences in perception are found, it is persuasive that students would find long readings more taxing on the iPad Mini than on larger size models or other media with larger font sizes. It would not be recommended to use mobile devices for content better transmitted by print media or larger screens, if available. Yet it has been observed that not a few students would prefer their smartphone over the iPad if the same function could be performed by the smaller device, which is more essential to them in everyday life. In any case it is widely recognized, by the students as well, that fluency with such technologies including mobile devices and personal computers along with English makes the students generally efficient and employable in contemporary society.

The chapter discussed many other issues such as criteria for sustainability of technologies, including usability and robustness. The demand for some functions will continue because they serve perennial human needs. Social media have served the need to connect to other people with increasing ease of use, while the devices and infrastructure afford an increasingly immediate and seamless connection to both content, whether informative or entertaining, and to people around the world.

The last case study concerned blended learning and flipped classrooms utilizing mobile devices. Blended learning has long been a mainstream practice in higher education, thought to be preferable to traditional classroom offline learning where interactions take place only where students and teachers can assemble in person, as well as to wholly online courses where students do not have the affordances of face-to-face guidance or hands-on activities utilizing university facilities. Internet content and communication is strategically blended to supplement the education of students fortunate enough to be enrolled in schools or universities with Internet connectivity and accumulated expertise in e-Learning technology and pedagogy. Flipped classrooms are a more recent development, a form of blended learning that takes advantage of online affordances to move the lecture aspect of classes to homework, such as by recording and assigning videos to watch, freeing the face-to-face class for discussions and other more interactive activities.

Chapter 5 detailed the array of specific technologies used by a nonnative English speaking professor to immerse students in English and improve their proficiency as measured by standardized tests, showing large increases from previous iterations of similar classes after introducing blended and flipped assignments. Some of the technologies were purchased from educational software vendors, while the open Web was accessed for TED Talks and other media to flip the classroom. The technologies could be utilized either on campus computers or while students were on the go. However, in line with the topic of this book, technologies were selected that could be accessed by the smartphones or other mobile devices which all students had readily available. Aoyama Gakuin University was a pioneer in m-Learning, and the earliest publication reported was by Dias (2002) at the same university (discussed and listed in the References under Chap. 1). Chapter 5 reported that all students in one seminar used an iPad as well as a smartphone for the course assignments. According to the methodology introduced in Chap. 1, blended learning is properly associated with e-Learning, which remains the umbrella concept, for one reason because m-Learning subsists on the university infrastructure for e-Learning.

Chapter 5 complements the other chapters with theoretical support for m-Learning and a sampling of the limitless affordances already available. CALL and MALL are interwoven with leading theories of language learning and motivation thereof to make sure that the pedagogy leads the technology in practice. The small screen size issue recurring in many studies is countered in this chapter by the idea that mobile phone users tend to have one app running at a time and may more sharply focus on a learning task as compared with the distractions or inefficiency of multitasking, since user attention can actually be focused on only one task at a time. Besides reporting on research showing the efficacy of blended learning, the chapter asserts that social learning is being rediscovered and reaching new heights with the confluence of mobile phones and social media. Open educational resources, courseware, and so forth are also seen as part of the robust new landscape for learning languages, connecting people and knowledge more and more efficiently.

Empirical assessment, showing significant increases in TOEIC scores and positive student feedback, provided evidence that blended learning, with freely available online TED Talks and e-Learning systems such as Newton m-Learning, the ATR CALL BRIX program, and Globalvoice CALL in the campus infrastructure, with a particular view to making such learning resources available to students' mobile phones and tablets, when guided by sociocultural pedagogy and blended into EFL courses systematically, constituted an effective approach to improve students' English proficiency.

The purpose of this brief book was not to prove that certain technologies ought to be adopted regardless of the context but rather to encourage thought and embolden experimentation available with a campus infrastructure and the devices students reach for first, at least in Japan. After seeing the wide range of approaches and a pedagogy that respects the cultural contours of students, if readers can make better informed choices for the future of their institutions, the purpose of this book will be accomplished.

FSC
www.fsc.org
MIX
Papier | Fördert gute Waldnutzung
FSC® C083411

Kolibri 360 GmbH
Ferdinand-Jühlke-Straße 7
99095 Erfurt, Deutschland
produktsicherheit@kolibri360.de